Be Set
Free!

How to overcome
**the performance trap,
condemnation and guilt**
to experience
God's grace and acceptance

PAUL M. GEISLER

© 2019 by Paul M. Geisler

Print ISBN: 978-1-54396-814-9

eBook ISBN: 978-1-54396-815-6

Thomas, Robert. *New American Standard Exhaustive Concordance of the Bible*. Holman, 1981.

Vine, W.E. *An Expository Dictionary of NT Words*. Revell, 1966.

Robertson, A.T. *Word Pictures in the New Testament IV*. Harper, 1931.

Reference to *The Free Dictionary* is from thefreedictionary.com. Accessed on 2/20/19. Used by permission.

Cover design by Bryan Dworshak, Convey Studio.

To my sons Grahm and Wynn.

May you always know the grace and power of God.

TABLE OF CONTENTS

INTRODUCTION

Therefore there is now no condemnation for
those who are in Christ Jesus (Rom. 8:1).

As a Christian, for too many years I suffered under condemnation and a subtle form of legalism. At the time of my salvation at age eight, I experienced plenty of the grace of God to come to the foot of the cross of Jesus and receive the free gift of forgiveness of sins that He offered me. But for many years after I came to the cross and into adulthood, I found myself living in a repeated cycle of sin, guilt, condemnation, judgment, rejection, confession and a frail restoration. I was taught that the Holy Spirit convicted me of sin and that when I sin, I am out of fellowship with God, or at least that He is out of fellowship with me. I was taught that this fellowship is restored only through confession. I was always walking on thin ice, knowing that at any time the conviction of a sin might come on me and crush me.

I thought that God was not pleased with me and that I should be spiritually "doing better." When I prayed, I came groveling to the Father with my constant admissions that I was not doing as well as I should be spiritually and that I likely had sinned that day in some unknown way. When I read the Bible, I thought it was up to me to get a blessing out of it. But when I read it, I often felt worse because of how I believed I was not measuring up to what it instructed. When I read passages of Jesus condemning the Pharisees, I felt like He was speaking to me. I felt like God was never quite happy or satisfied with my spiritual performance. I thought that I could be praying more, reading my Bible more, witnessing more to nonbelievers, or leading a discipleship group.

I sometimes participated in ministries in the church because I thought that's what I *should* be doing or because I felt guilty if I did not. Prayer meetings especially bored me. I tried to avoid them when they were tacked on to the end of a small group meeting. In the eight-year period after college, I was completely burned out and stopped volunteering for any ministries in the church.

During this time, I went through repeated cycles of trying to grow spiritually, giving up, and then trying again. The message in my head was clear—I was not measuring up to God's expectations of me, and in order for God to be pleased with me, I needed to be more sin-free and I needed to be doing more for the Lord. This subtle form of legalism had a devastating negative impact on me. It kept me from living the abundant life that God promised. It certainly was not a picture of the victorious Christian life.

This cycle of condemnation and performance continued until I was 30 years old in 1992. I was in a performance trap and I couldn't find my way out. At that time, I finally told God, "I quit!" I told God that I was unable to grow spiritually based on my own efforts and that if I was ever going to grow spiritually, He was going to have to do it. I was serious. I was done! I still trusted in Jesus for salvation, but I stopped all efforts to get closer to Him through prayer and reading the Bible. He brought me to a place where I finally recognized that I was absolutely spiritually empty and in my own strength I had no ability to do anything for Him. I had no desire to pray or to serve Him in any way. I kept showing up at church every week, hoping that I would hear something that was the missing truth that would free and transform me.

In God's sovereign timing, about a week after I quit, a friend introduced me to a Christian counselor who explained biblical truths about grace that, unfortunately, I had never heard in church. I met with him for a period of time and also studied and searched the word diligently for the truth. I finally came to new conclusions about God's love, grace and forgiveness. I was set free!

The change in my life was dramatic, and I have never been the same since. The heavy load of guilt and condemnation I had been carrying all my life was lifted. I was no longer on the spiritual treadmill of performance. For the first time since I had been saved at the age of eight, I experienced great joy in my salvation. I understood how awesome salvation and forgiveness really were. I was fully accepted by God!

I believe this new understanding opened the door to receive much more power of the Holy Spirit in my life. I began to see Him minister to others through me in power and ways I would not have imagined before. Before I learned about grace, I was entirely ineffective in prayer. But the Lord gave me new spiritual gifts that mainly centered around the gift of intercession. How ironic—here I now was able to effectively intercede for others after having felt so unable to intercede in my own strength for all those years. I shared the truths I learned about grace with other believers. As God led me to pray for them, I saw Him set them free also! I have now been living in freedom and power for 26 years.

If you identify with this cycle of condemnation or performance, then this book is for you. The key to being set free is to know the truth about grace. Jesus said, "You will know the truth and the truth will set you free" (John 8:32). Therefore, I am going to rely heavily on the word of God to speak for itself. We will see what it says about our forgiveness and righteousness in Christ. We will learn how to be set free from the cycle of condemnation and judgment. My prayer is that you will experience the acceptance and freedom that Jesus offers as well as how to walk in His power. I invite you to walk with me through the truths in God's word that set me free. Brother or Sister, it is time for you to Be Set Free!

CHAPTER 1

No Condemnation

She was covered in shame, guilt and humiliation. Her moral failure was exposed to what felt like the whole world. She had been caught in the act of adultery by no less than the religious leaders. They had brought her into the temple and placed her in the center of a crowd that was listening to some man teach. The rulers were all in agreement that their law said she should be executed by stoning and that it should be done now.

They had brought her to Jesus to test him to see what he would say. But she likely didn't know who Jesus was. From the woman's viewpoint, all of them were in agreement about her stoning. But, for some reason, they asked one last person for his consent in the matter before her fate was sealed. Surely this plainly clothed person would not disagree with the religious leaders or dispute their authority. This seemed to be only a formality.

They asked Him how He would judge in her case, but He did not answer. He only stooped to the ground to write something unknown in the dirt. How long would He delay in giving His consent also for her death? There was no question that she was guilty. The law was clear that adultery was wrong and punishable by death. Her shame and humiliation were complete.

Finally, when they pressed Him, He stood up and said to them, "He who is without sin among you, let him be the first to throw a stone at her" (John 8:7). His response was shocking. Who was he to suggest not following the law?

The religious leaders, knowing that they were also sinners, started leaving one by one, the older ones first, until no one was left. She couldn't believe that they had all left.

Who was this man who had such spiritual authority that with *one sentence* he was able to convince the religious leaders to discard their law that had been established for over a thousand years?

"Jesus then said to her, 'Woman, where are they? Did no one condemn you?' She said, 'No one, Lord.' And Jesus said, 'I do not condemn you, either. Go. From now on sin no more'" (John 8:10–11).

How could he extend such grace to her? This was new and unprecedented. Who was he? He first extended grace to her, and then *after* that He encouraged her to walk away from her pattern of sin. Paul says in Romans 2:4, "[T]he kindness of God leads you to repentance." This is what Jesus was doing with her. He spoke peace into a situation that was very volatile and peace and forgiveness into the woman's life.

In order for us to understand the grace that Jesus offers us today, we must first look at the foundation of grace that He offers us in salvation.

Grace in Salvation

Jesus now gives us a right relationship with God by faith in Himself and His sacrificial work on the cross. Because of His great love for us, He died to pay the penalty for our sins. He knew that it was a debt that we were unable to pay.

This is a free gift that He offers us. The Apostle Paul said, "For the wages of sin is death, but the free gift of God is eternal life in Christ Jesus our Lord" (Rom. 6:23). We receive it simply by faith.

Paul says, "For by grace you have been saved through faith; and that not of yourselves, it is the gift of God; not as a result of works, so that no one may boast" (Eph. 2:8–9).

Paul makes two statements here about what DOES save us: we are saved by grace through faith, and it is the gift of God. He also makes two statements here about what does NOT save us: it is not of ourselves, and it is not as a result of works, so that no one may boast.

Salvation is not something that we can obtain through our own works. God knew our helpless state, and, in His great love for us, He gave it to us as a free gift. We just need to receive it. There is no work in receiving a gift.

Jesus could not have stated the requirement for salvation any clearer than in John 5:24, where he proclaims: "Truly, truly, I say to you, he who hears My word, and believes Him who sent Me, has eternal life, and does not come into judgment, but has passed out of death into life."

There are no works here. The requirement is that we believe that God the Father sent his son Jesus into the world. The result is eternal life! We might like to make it more complicated than that by adding works to it because pride and self-righteousness can keep us from receiving free gifts. It takes humility to receive a gift from someone and not believe we are obligated to return the favor. But, with God, the gift He gives us is so large that there is no way we could ever repay it. All we can do is receive it with humility and thankfulness.

Again, Jesus makes it clear that simple belief is all that is needed: "Therefore they said to Him, 'What shall we do, so that we may work the works of God?' Jesus answered and said to them, 'This is the work of God, that you believe in Him whom He has sent'" (John 6:28–29). It is only faith in Jesus that saves us. In the New

Testament, the word "faith" or "believe" is given as the only requirement for salvation 57 times.[1]

Jesus asks us to believe in (trust in) the One whom God His Father has sent into the world. God sent Him into the world to be the savior of the world. Jesus is inviting us to accept Him as coming from the Father and to trust in Him for salvation. John says, "But as many as received Him, to them He gave the right to become children of God, even to those who believe in His name" (John 1:12).

Jesus died for all sins for all people for all time by His one act. Peter says, "For Christ also died for sins once for all, the just for the unjust, so that He might bring us to God, having been put to death in the flesh, but made alive in the spirit" (1 Pet. 3:18).

Some may say, "but Jesus said you must enter through the narrow gate. Therefore, salvation is difficult." This is a reference to where Jesus says, "Enter through the narrow gate; for the gate is wide and the way is broad that leads to destruction, and there are many who enter through it. For the gate is small and the way is narrow that leads to life, and there are few who find it" (Matt. 7:13–14).

But Jesus *is* the narrow gate. John says, "So Jesus said to them again, 'Truly, truly, I say to you, I am the door of the sheep. All who came before Me are thieves and robbers, but the sheep did not hear them. I am the door; if anyone enters through Me, he will be saved, and will go in and out and find pasture'" (John 10:7–9). Just because the gate is narrow, meaning the method of salvation is very specific, doesn't mean it is not simple. Jesus *is* the narrow gate, and salvation

---

1   Luke 7:50; 8:13; John 1:7, 12; 3:15, 16, 18; 5:24; 6:35, 40, 47; 7:38–39; 8:24; 11:25, 26; 20:31; Acts 8:37; 10:43; 13:38–39; 15:7–9, 16:31; 26:17–18; Rom. 1:16–17; 3:21–22, 26, 28, 30; 4:3, 5, 11, 24; 5:1, 2; 9:30, 32; 10:4, 6, 9–10; 1 Cor. 1:21; 2 Cor. 4:13-14; Gal. 2:15–16; 3:2, 8, 22, 26; 5:5; Eph. 1:13, 2:8–9; 3:12, 17; Phil. 3:9; Col. 1:21–23; Heb. 6:12; 10:39; 1 Pet. 1:5, 9; 1 John 5:13.

is simple. Jesus also reinforced that He is the narrow way when He said, "I am the way, and the truth, and the life; no one comes to the Father but through Me" (John 14:6).

He Gives Us His Righteousness

Jesus took our sin upon Himself on the cross. Paul says, "He made Him who knew no sin to be sin on our behalf, so that we might become the righteousness of God in Him" (2 Cor. 5:21). In exchange for our sins, we are given the gift of His righteousness. God credits righteousness to us through faith. Paul says, "But to the one who does not work, but believes in Him who justifies the ungodly, his faith is credited as righteousness, just as David also speaks of the blessing on the man to whom God credits righteousness apart from works: 'Blessed are those whose lawless deeds have been forgiven, And whose sins have been covered'" (Rom. 4:5–7).

Adam's original sin in Genesis brought sin and death to the human race. But Jesus now brings righteousness and life to us. Paul says, "For if by the transgression of the one, death reigned through the one, much more those who receive the abundance of grace and of the gift of righteousness will reign in life through the One, Jesus Christ. So then as through one transgression there resulted condemnation to all men, even so through one act of righteousness there resulted justification of life to all men" (Rom 5:17–18).

We receive this gift of righteousness from God through faith, not through our works. Paul says, "I count all things to be lost . . . so that I may gain Christ, and may be found in Him, not having a righteousness of my own derived from the Law, but that which is through faith in Christ, the righteousness which comes from God on the basis of faith" (Phil. 3:8–9).

Righteousness does not come through the law, but it does come through faith in Jesus. Paul says, "I do not nullify the grace of God, for if righteousness comes through the Law, then Christ died needlessly" (Gal. 2:21).

No Wrath of God for the Believer

Under grace, we are no longer recipients of the wrath of God. Paul says, "Much more then, having now been justified by His blood, we shall be saved from the wrath of God through Him" (Rom. 5:9).

Because of Jesus' substitution for us on the cross, all of the wrath of God for our sins was placed on Him and we received His righteousness. Wow, what a great deal for us! It seems like this is too good to be true. But a God who loves us without limits would do such a thing. And He did it while we were still sinners. Paul says, "But God demonstrates His own love toward us, in that while we were yet sinners, Christ died for us" (Rom. 5:8). If you ever wanted proof that God loves you, this is it.

If you trust in Jesus, then God does not have any remaining anger or wrath at your sin! It has all been dealt with on the cross. For God to still have wrath for your sin, you would have to be in a state of not being saved. Your sin is what separated you from God, and He has dealt with that problem on the cross.

When you sin, there is no remaining wrath or anger of God towards you if you trust in Jesus. It has all been paid for by Him on the cross. If we think we need to grovel or somehow owe God for our sin, then we are diminishing the work that Jesus did on the cross.

His work is complete. Jesus said on the cross right before he died, "It is finished" (John 19:30), which was an accounting term meaning "paid in full." Your debt was not partially paid. Your sins—your debt—have been paid in full by Jesus on the cross. There is no more sacrifice to be made. There is no work that you can do to add to the work of Jesus to get yourself saved or forgiven. You have obtained the righteousness of Jesus as a free gift.

Here's the bottom line. All of your sins past, present and future were laid on Jesus when he died on the cross. Therefore, all of God's anger and wrath were taken by Jesus for you on the cross. He died in your place. Isaiah prophesied about Jesus's sacrifice in Isaiah 53:6 where he said: "We all, like sheep, have gone astray, each of us has turned to our own way; and the Lord has laid on him the iniquity of us all."

CHAPTER 2

The Law Is Fulfilled in Us

The law in the Old Testament is a list of over 600 commands given to the Jewish people. The law was given so that we would recognize that we are sinners and can never be perfect on our own effort. Paul says, "What shall we say then? Is the Law sin? May it never be! On the contrary, I would not have come to know sin except through the Law; for I would not have known about coveting if the Law had not said, 'You shall not covet'" (Rom. 7:7).

The law put a magnifying glass on the fact that we are sinners. Paul says, "The Law came in so that the transgression would increase" (Rom. 5:19). Really? Why would God give us something so that we could become greater sinners? It is because the law shows us our moral helplessness.

Jesus summarized the law by saying we should love God and love our neighbor. Matthew records, "One of them, a lawyer, asked Him a question, testing Him, 'Teacher, which is the great commandment in the Law?' And He said to him, 'You shall love the Lord your God with all your heart, and with all your soul, and with all your mind.' The second is like it, 'You shall love your neighbor as yourself.' On these two commandments depend the whole Law and the Prophets" (Matt. 22:35–37). Both of these are tall orders that none of us can perfectly follow.

The Jews, as instructed in the law, sacrificed animals as an atonement for their sins. But this was only a foreshadow or symbol of Jesus who was to come. He is the Lamb of God who took away all sins for all time. John the Baptist knew that this was Jesus' mission.

The Apostle John gives the account, "The next day he saw Jesus coming to him and said, 'Behold, the Lamb of God who takes away the sin of the world!'" (John 1:29). Peter says, "For Christ also died for sins once for all, the just for the unjust, so that He might bring us to God, having been put to death in the flesh, but made alive in the spirit" (1 Pet. 3:18).

It is not enough for us to be sin-free (which is not possible) because we are all "in Adam." Adam sinned, and the human race is fallen and needs redemption (Rom. 5:18).

The law only shows us how we are failing and brings death. Paul says, "I was once alive apart from the Law; but when the commandment came, sin became alive and I died" (Rom. 7:9). The law cannot bring us real life. Paul says, "For if a law had been given which was able to impart life, then righteousness would indeed have been based on law" (Gal. 3:21).

Jesus Was the First to Fulfill the Law

God gave the law to show us that no one is perfect and that we needed a way to be redeemed. We need God himself to do for us what we are powerless to do. We need a savior who can save us when we are unable to save ourselves.

Since no one was able to keep the law perfectly, God sent his son Jesus to do it. Jesus said of himself, "Do not think that I came to abolish the Law or the Prophets; I did not come to abolish but to fulfill" (Matt. 5:17). He fulfilled the law as originally given by God, obeying it perfectly and living the first-ever sinless life.

God Gives Us Righteousness and New Life in the Spirit

God has introduced a new way for us to be righteous apart from living up to a law that we could never live up to. The new way of obtaining righteousness is through faith in Jesus. Paul says, "But now apart from the Law the righteousness of God has been manifested, being witnessed by the Law and the Prophets, even the righteousness of God through faith in Jesus Christ for all those who believe; for there is no distinction; for all have sinned and fall short of the glory of God, being justified as a gift by His grace through the redemption which is in Christ Jesus" (Rom. 3:21–24).

God looks at us as ones who have met the righteous requirements of the law. He has ushered in a new way of living for us that is by the Spirit and not by the law. The requirements of the law are now fulfilled in us so that we can live under the direction of the Spirit rather than by the letter of the law. Paul says, "For the law of the Spirit of life in Christ Jesus has set you free from the law of sin and of death. For what the Law could not do, weak as it was through the flesh, God did: sending His own Son in the likeness of sinful flesh and as an offering for sin, He condemned sin in the flesh, so that the requirement of the Law might be fulfilled in us, who do not walk according to the flesh but according to the Spirit" (Rom. 8:2–4). God made one offering for sin to give us righteousness. The writer of Hebrews says, "For by one offering He has perfected for all time those who are sanctified" (Heb. 10:14).

A set of rules could never give us new life on the inside. Rules are only external. We need to be made new from the inside out. Because of this, Jesus gives us new life on the inside when His Spirit lives in us. Jesus said, "He who believes in Me, as the Scripture said, 'From his innermost being will flow rivers of living water.'" (John

7:38). And He says, "I came that they may have life, and have it abundantly" (John 10:10). He also says, "It is the Spirit who gives life; the flesh profits nothing; the words that I have spoken to you are spirit and are life" (John 6:63). Paul says that we are now adequate in serving God by the Spirit (instead of the old way of serving by the law), "who also made us adequate as servants of a new covenant, not of the letter but of the Spirit; for the letter kills, but the Spirit gives life" (2 Cor. 3:6).

God set aside the old system of the law and replaced it with the new way of grace in Jesus. John says, "For the Law was given through Moses; grace and truth were realized through Jesus Christ" (John 1:7). Because Jesus fulfilled the law for us, we are no longer under the law. Paul says, "[F]or the Law brings about wrath, but where there is no law, there also is no violation" (Rom 4:15). He also says, "For Christ is the end of the law for righteousness to everyone who believes" (Rom. 10:4) and "But if you are led by the Spirit, you are not under the Law" (Gal. 5:18).

The Law Is a Tutor

The law was a temporary system that God put in place until he revealed the better way of living by the Spirit. Paul says, "But before faith came, we were kept in custody under the law, being shut up to the faith which was later to be revealed. Therefore, the Law has become our tutor to lead us to Christ, so that we may be justified by faith. But now that faith has come, we are no longer under a tutor. For you are all sons of God through faith in Christ Jesus" (Gal. 3:23–26). From A.T. Robertson's *Word Pictures of the New Testament*, the word "tutor" here is the word for a slave in Greek and Roman families who was in charge of a boy from about six to sixteen. He watched the boy's behavior at home and attended him when he went away from home to school. Paul in Galatians is saying that the law was a tutor to lead us to Christ. It was temporary, with God's ultimate goal that we would be justified by faith in Jesus. Once faith came through Jesus, there was no longer any need for the tutor.

As an illustration of this, a friend of mine had a rule for his son that he was not allowed to punch his sister. That was an age-appropriate rule for a boy. But when the boy grew up to be a young man, my friend hoped that his son's love for his sister would guide his behavior rather than the childhood rule. The childhood rule for the boy was like a tutor and was temporary until the boy developed a better way that was internal. This is the difference between living under the law and living under the new way of grace.

Is This Enough?

These first two chapters laid a foundation for a theology of grace. Years ago, I could have heard all of this and still not have been fundamentally set free. That was because there were two remaining things I had been taught in church that were central to my being kept in bondage under a subtle form of legalism. If these two beliefs had not been corrected, then I never would have been transformed. We will take a look at the first belief in chapter 3 and the second in chapter 4.

CHAPTER 3

Conviction of Sin

I had been taught that the Holy Spirit convicts us of sin, and you may have learned that also. *The Free Dictionary* definitions of "convict" are as follows:

1. *Law* To find or prove (someone) guilty of an offense or crime, especially by the verdict of a court:
2. To show or declare to be blameworthy; condemn:
3. To make aware of one's sinfulness or guilt.

In the light of grace, this belief of conviction by the Holy Spirit needs further scrutiny.

There is only one passage in the New Testament that says that the Holy Spirit has the role of convicting anyone of sin, and it is in John 16:7-11, where Jesus said, "But I tell you the truth, it is to your advantage that I go away; for if I do not go away, the Helper will not come to you; but if I go, I will send Him to you. And He, when He comes, will convict the world concerning sin and righteousness and judgment; concerning sin, because they do not believe in Me; and concerning righteousness, because I go to the Father and you no longer see Me; and concerning judgment, because the ruler of this world has been judged."

Who Is The World?

The Holy Spirit convicts "the world" regarding sin and righteousness and judgment. Who is Jesus referring to when he says "the world?" Is this everyone in the world, including both believers and nonbelievers? We can let the passage interpret itself when Jesus follows by saying, "concerning sin, because *they do not believe in me*" (John 16:9, emphasis mine). "The world," in this case, is referring to unbelievers!

Jesus again uses "the world" to refer to unbelievers 12 verses later in verse 20: "Truly, truly, I say to you, that you will weep and lament, but *the world* will rejoice; you will grieve, but your grief will be turned into joy" (John 16:20, emphasis mine). Again, in the next chapter Jesus prays, "[F]or the words which You gave Me I have given to them; and they received them and truly understood that I came forth from You, and they believed that You sent Me. I ask on their behalf; I do not ask on behalf of *the world*, but of those whom You have given Me; for they are Yours" (John 17:8–9, emphasis mine). In these second and third passages, the context also clearly indicates that "the world" is referring to nonbelievers. In addition, "the world" in all three passages comes from the same Greek root word *kosmos*.

Sin

If we go back to John 16:8, when Jesus said, "And He, when He comes, will convict the world concerning sin," He is saying that the Holy Spirit convicts the unbelieving world of their sin so that they will recognize that they need a savior. The solution to the sin problem is to "believe in me" (John 16:9). As we have seen earlier, salvation is through simple faith in Jesus to save us.

Righteousness

Jesus said the Holy Spirit also convicts the world regarding righteousness, "because I go to the Father and you no longer see Me" (John 16:10). While Jesus was on earth, He was the only sinless person. If people wanted to know what righteousness looked like, they just needed to see Jesus. After Jesus left, there was no perfect person to see. So, the Holy Spirit convicts the unbelieving world of what righteousness is so that they come to salvation.

Judgment

Lastly, the Holy Spirit convicts the world regarding judgment, "because the ruler of this world has been judged" (John 16:11). Satan was the ruler of the world as seen in the temptation of Jesus (Matt. 4). Satan has been judged, and the Holy Spirit is convicting the unbelieving world that a judgment day is also coming for them that they should prepare for.

Revelation of Sin

"The world" (John 16:8) is the unbelieving world, and the Holy Spirit convicts it of sin, righteousness and judgment, all to show the world that it needs salvation.

Prior to my being set free from my misconceptions, I had a wrong interpretation of this passage that caused me untold destruction in my life. It kept me in a repeated state of condemnation, discouragement and fleeing from the presence of God.

I believe that there is a way that the Holy Spirit sometimes reveals sin to me but that it does not come to me with judgment, condemnation or guilt. It's as though a lightbulb of truth turns on in my head. I finally see something as not in alignment with God's moral will (sin). It comes as a gentle revelation of the truth. It is certainly not the Holy Spirit "convicting" me. It is more like changing to having more of the mind of Christ. We don't always see everything as He does. The more we see from God's perspective on reality, the more we will have a revelation of what is sin. This is becoming more like Christ.

One passage that might support this view of a gentle revelation is when Paul says, "And do not be conformed to this world, but be transformed by the renewing of your mind, so that you may prove what the will of God is, that which is good and acceptable and perfect" (Rom. 12:2). But we need to hold on tightly to the truth that there is no judgment of the Holy Spirit towards us!

Holy Spirit as Helper

Furthermore, every place in the New Testament that talks about the role of the Holy Spirit in the life of the believer mentions a way in which He overtly builds up or helps the believer. Here are a few examples of the roles of the Holy Spirit toward us. The Holy Spirit

- is our helper (John 14:26);
- is our comforter (Acts 9:31);
- gives us strength and power (Acts 1:8; Eph. 3:16);
- gives us life (John 6:63);
- abides with us and is in us (John 14:17);
- is a gift to us (Acts 2:38);
- gives us hope (Rom. 15:13);
- gives us wisdom (Col. 1:9);

- gives us what to say (Matt. 10:20); and
- makes us born again (John 3:5).

Satan as the Accuser

On the other hand, Satan has a very different role and objective in the life of a believer. One of the roles is that he is our accuser. Revelations 12:10, speaking of Satan, says, "[F]or the accuser of our brethren has been thrown down, he who accuses them before our God day and night." That is amazing. Satan accuses us of sin before the Father nonstop. So why would the Holy Spirit also have this role of accusing us?

The truth is that Satan is our accuser and the Holy Spirit is not, but is *for* us. Paul says, "What then shall we say to these things? If God is for us, who is against us?" (Rom. 8:31). Actually, it is Satan who is against us.

For years, when I experienced conviction, I assumed it was the Holy Spirit impressing it on me. But the Bible says that it is only Satan who accuses us. How could the Holy Spirit be in agreement with what Satan is doing and be doing the same thing?

On the other hand, Jesus told some nonbelievers that Satan was their father. He said of them, "You are of your father the devil, and you want to do the desires of your father" (John 8:44). So for a nonbeliever, Satan has been described as their father but the Holy Spirit is their convictor of sin (for their benefit so that they can come to salvation). At the point of salvation, the roles of Satan and the Holy Spirit are reversed in a person's life. Satan becomes the accuser, and the Holy Spirit becomes the Advocate and Helper in so many ways.

The Big Deception

How could Satan possibly convince me that he was the Holy Spirit? Paul says, "[F]or even Satan disguises himself as an angel of light" (2 Cor. 11:14). Even more tragic is that the only time I really thought that God was speaking to me was when I was convicted of sin. It was only Satan the whole time! Jesus talked about Satan this way when he said, "The thief comes only to steal and kill and destroy; I came that they may have life, and have it abundantly" (John 10:10).

For believers, the Holy Spirit is *for* us and Satan is *against* us. This is a huge deception that Satan had me convinced of for many years. He actually had me thinking that he was the Holy Spirit giving me conviction of sin. This new understanding was the first of two keys that set me free.

CHAPTER FOUR

Confession of Sin

This is the second of two significant beliefs that I had to reevaluate in order to fully know and experience God's freedom. I was taught that when I sin, I need to confess that sin to God in order to receive forgiveness and restore fellowship with Him. The only New Testament passage that is postresurrection (in the new era of grace) where we are told to confess our sins to God is in 1 John 1:9: "If we confess our sins, He is faithful and righteous to forgive us our sins and to cleanse us from all unrighteousness."

Verse by Itself

Let's first look at this verse in 1 John by itself, and then we will look at the verse in its context.

First, when are we actually "cleansed from *all* unrighteousness?" It is at the point of salvation when we trust in Jesus! Jesus says, "He who believes in the Son has eternal life; but he who does not obey the Son will not see life, but the wrath of God abides on him" (John 3:36). Also, He says, "Truly, truly, I say to you, he who hears My word, and believes Him who sent Me, has eternal life, and does not come into judgment, but has passed out of death into life" (John 5:24). In these two verses, the ones who believe in Jesus (at the time of belief) have eternal life and do not come under judgment. The ones who do not believe in Him have the wrath of God still on them, will come into judgment and are still in a state of death.

Second, if we were to sin and not confess it, then 1 John 1:9 would tell us that we are NOT cleansed from all unrighteousness, which would mean that we are in a state of nonsalvation. But keeping up with every last sin that we commit would be impossible since there are likely sins we are committing that we are not aware of. Also, it says that He is faithful to forgive our sins when we confess them. So, what if we as believers did not confess one sin that we were aware of or we were to die one hour before we would have confessed it? Would that mean that He has not forgiven us and we are then not saved? This is not a reasonable interpretation.

So, for the two reasons above, when we look at this verse on confession by itself, it makes no sense to interpret it as a practice for the believer.

Verse in Context

Furthermore, let's look at the context of 1 John 1:9 to see what it is talking about. John is comparing two types of people in the first chapter (and also somewhat through the rest of the book). He uses the word "we" many times and refers to two different groups with it. We need to determine exactly who these two groups are that he is comparing. One helpful way to do that is to list the individual characteristics of each of the two groups. Then we can read the complete description of each and try to determine who they are. Below is the text from chapter 1, verses 6–10 except for verse 9. After we understand the groups before and after verse 9, we will revisit this one verse.

Group A:
6 "If we say that we have fellowship with Him and yet walk in the darkness, we lie and do not practice the truth[.]"

8 "If we say that we have no sin, we are deceiving ourselves and the truth is not in us."
10 "If we say that we have not sinned, we make Him a liar and His word is not in us."

Group B:
7 "[B]ut if we walk in the Light as He Himself is in the Light, we have fellowship with one another, and the blood of Jesus His Son cleanses us from all sin."

There is a great contrast between these two groups. Group A say they are not sinners and are lying about it to themselves (v. 8) and to others (v. 6). They make God out to be a liar about it (v. 10) because God says they are sinners but they believe they are not. Paul says, "[F]or all have sinned and fall short of the glory of God" (Rom. 3:23).

Group A also have the characteristics of walking in darkness, not practicing the truth, having no truth in them and not having His word in them. Concerning their "walking in darkness," the Apostle Paul talks about the difference between a saved and unsaved person this way: "[F]or you were formerly darkness, but now you are Light in the Lord; walk as children of Light" (Eph. 5:8). Also, concerning Group A in verse 10 that "His word is not in us," this is the same phrase used to describe a nonbeliever when Jesus says "You do not have His word abiding in you, for you do not believe Him whom He sent" (John 5:38).

Group B is characterized as walking in the light, having fellowship with one another and, most importantly, having the blood of Jesus cleanse them from all sin.

I submit to you that Group A is not saved and Group B is. I am not saying that John believes that the recipients of his letter are unsaved, but for the purposes of teaching, he is describing a group of people who are not saved. He makes it clear in the rest of his book by the way he speaks to his readers that he believes they are saved (1 John 2:12–13; 5:13). Group A would not admit that they were sinners. Thus, they would not see a need for a savior. Group B knows they are sinners, and they alone have the blood of Jesus cleansing them from ALL sin.

If this is the case, that Group A is not saved and Group B is, then let's now look at the verse we left out of the context of 1 John 1.

9 "If we confess our sins, He is faithful and righteous to forgive us our sins and to cleanse us from all unrighteousness."

I also submit to you that this verse is telling us how to transition from Group A to Group B. It is a salvation verse! It is not a verse for the believer to be practicing regularly. Salvation is a one-time event. Verse 9 is talking about a one-time event when we are cleansed from ALL sin. Verse 9 acknowledges that the unsaved Group A need to confess their sin (in verses 6, 8 and 10 they denied they were sinners), and then they become a part of Group B, who have had the blood of Jesus cleanse them from all sin (v. 7).

Verse in Larger Context

Now we will take an even larger look at the context. John finishes his introduction to this letter in verse 4. Then he starts his main first teaching in verse 5 by explaining some elementary principles of spiritual truth when he says, "This is the message we have heard from Him and announce to you, that God is Light, and in Him there is no darkness at all" (1 John 1:5). It doesn't get much simpler than this. He is declaring that 1) there is a God, 2) He is all good and 3) there is no evil in Him. These are the ABCs of theology. He continues with his basic teaching by explaining that many believe (in error) that they are not sinners, and then he explains the method of salvation in verse 9 where he says that if we confess our sins, He will forgive us.

King David

What about King David wasting away when he had not yet confessed his sin with Bathsheba to God (Psalm 32:3)? This was the Old Testament era of the law when God dealt differently with His people. There were various times specified in the law that they were required to confess sins and make animal sacrifices. But Jesus has fulfilled the law for us. We are now living in the New Testament era where God is dealing differently with mankind.

The writer of Hebrews talks about the difference between the old and new periods and argues the differences with a prophecy from Jeremiah 31:31–33:

For by one offering He has perfected for all time those who are sanctified. And the Holy Spirit also testifies to us; for after saying,

"This is the covenant that I will make with them
After those days, says the Lord:
I will put My laws upon their heart,
And on their mind I will write them,"
He then says,
"And their sins and their lawless deeds
I will remember no more."

Now where there is forgiveness of these things, there is no
longer any offering for sin (Heb. 10:14–18).

First, the writer of Hebrews says we have been "perfected for
all time." This is a once-and-done event that Jesus accomplished for
us on the cross which we receive through faith in Him. In this new
era, we don't have the written law anymore to guide us, but He has
placed His laws on our hearts. We are now guided by our conscience
and the internal leading of the Spirit rather than by the external letter of the law.

But the most radical statement here is where Jeremiah says of
the new era that God will remember our sins no more. In the Old
Testament there were various times where God's anger burned at the
people because of their sin (Num. 11:1; Josh. 7:1). Jeremiah is saying
this doesn't happen in the New Testament era because He remem-
bers our sins no more. This implies that He used to remember them.

This "remembering" of sins has the idea of lasting anger at the
sin and holding it against us. It's like a friend saying, "I won't for-
get what you did to me." They are vowing to hold a grudge and not
forgive you. But God "forgets" because He no longer has righteous
anger at your sin. It was dealt with on the cross.

The Lord's Prayer

Jesus said in the Lord's Prayer that we should pray, "And forgive us
our debts, as we also have forgiven our debtors" (Matt. 6:12). Does
this instruct us to confess our sins for forgiveness? Jesus goes on to
say something even more profound about forgiveness: "For if you
forgive others for their transgressions, your heavenly Father will also
forgive you. But if you do not forgive others, then your Father will

not forgive your transgressions" (Matt. 6:14–15). Will God not forgive our sins if we do not forgive others? Once again, these are statements that He made inside the Old Testament era of the law when God remembered sins and held them against people.

Jesus affirmed several times in Matthew 5 in the Sermon on the Mount that they were still in the era of the law. He did so first when He said, "Do not think that I came to abolish the Law or the Prophets; I did not come to abolish but to fulfill" (Matt. 5:17).

He affirmed it a second time when He said, "Whoever then annuls one of the least of these commandments, and teaches others to do the same, shall be called least in the kingdom of heaven; but whoever keeps and teaches them, he shall be called great in the kingdom of heaven" (Matt. 5:19).

Then He affirmed for a third time that they were still in the Old Testament era a few verses later when He spoke of what to do when performing sacrifices (an Old Testament law practice): "Therefore if you are presenting your offering at the altar, and there remember that your brother has something against you, leave your offering there before the altar and go; first be reconciled to your brother, and then come and present your offering" (Matt. 5:23–24).

There are different views on exactly when the new era of grace began, but it is commonly agreed that it did not start until at least the death of Jesus. Jesus was teaching His listeners how to pray in the era of law that they were in at the time when he was teaching.

One Verse

Going back to 1 John 1:9 (confession of sin), it is a commonly accepted practice of Bible interpretation to not base a doctrine on one verse in isolation. First John 1:9 has been used exactly in this way—in isolation—to argue that it should be a regular practice of believers to confess their sins for forgiveness, or at least to restore fellowship with the Father. There are no other verses in the New Testament era of grace that state this idea. But there is significant evidence that this is instead a salvation verse.

Feeling out of Fellowship

I have heard people say that they confess their sins because they feel out of fellowship with God. But the reality is that people *feel* out of fellowship because they *believe* they are out of fellowship. *Feelings* are the result of *beliefs* about *events*. The sequence is:

1. An event occurs,
2. We have a belief about that event and
3. Feelings result.

If an event happens and we believe the worst possible reason for that event, then we will have resulting feelings of hurt, fear, and so on. If we believe the best possible reason for the event, then we will not have these negative emotions.

For example, say I have a good friend whom I speak with often on the phone and one day I have a slight disagreement with him about something. The next time I call him, he doesn't pick up. I leave him a voicemail asking him to return my call. For four days, I don't hear from him, which is unusual in our relationship. I believe that he is upset with me and doesn't want to talk with me. I feel hurt and stressed over a strained relationship. Then after five days have gone by, he calls me and tells me that he lost his phone. He explains that he has had to buy a new phone and get his address list restored. He also says that he is not upset about our last conversation. I don't feel hurt any more over the strained relationship because there was no strain.

The original event in this story is that we had a disagreement and he did not subsequently return my call. The belief I had about the event was that he was snubbing me. I had resulting feelings of hurt. Once my belief about the event changed, then my resulting feelings became completely different.

This principle manifests itself in our relationship with God. We commit a sin (the event). Our belief is that we are guilty and that the sin has not been fully paid for and that God is upset with us. The resulting feelings are guilt and shame, which can also lead to the subsequent action of running from God and all sorts of other problems like anxiety, depression, substance abuse and so on. If we change our belief that when we sin God is not out of fellowship with us and He has no righteous anger at us because of sin, then we will not have the resulting feeling of being of out of fellowship with Him or the feeling of condemnation that comes with it.

Human Relationships

I have also heard it argued that we need to confess our sins to God because it's just like a human relationship where we offend someone and need to apologize to restore fellowship. There are a couple of problems with this view. First, God is not human and He does not exist inside time. All of your sins past, present and future have been placed on the cross, and He already sees them as paid for, so He has no righteous anger remaining about them.

The second problem with this view is that it is self-righteous. We think that we can keep track of our sins and that there aren't any that slip by us unnoticed. We don't understand the depth of our depravity. Isaiah 64:6 says, "And all our righteous deeds are like a filthy garment." It's not just all of our sins that need redemption, it's our entire being that needs redemption.

The traditional views of 1 John 1:9 (confession of sin) and John 16:8 (Holy Spirit conviction of sin) kept me in a never-ending cycle of condemnation, defeat and a subtle form of the law. Having a new understanding of these two verses were the major keys for me in experiencing freedom.

How Do We Live?

So, what do we do when we sin? We can thank God that He has forgiven us, and we can repent (turn from it) without coming under condemnation. We do not need to beg Him for forgiveness because we already have it in Jesus. We were crucified with him on the cross (Gal. 2:20).

James 5:16 gives the only legitimate way for us to confess sins now, and that is to each other: "Therefore, confess your sins to one another, and pray for one another so that you may be healed." There is certainly healing that we can experience when we are able to be honest about our failures and have someone unconditionally accept us. I have friends who live with a good understanding of grace, and it is healing for me to be able to tell them anything without fear of judgment. What an awesome way this is for the body of Christ to manifest His forgiveness and acceptance.

CHAPTER FIVE

Living under Grace

We are now free to live under grace with no condemnation! Paul says, "Therefore there is now no condemnation for those who are in Christ Jesus. For the law of the Spirit of life in Christ Jesus has set you free from the law of sin and of death" (Rom. 8:1–4). Do you think that God is condemning you every time you sin? He is not! You are no longer under condemnation. Do you still condemn yourself? God is no longer condemning us, so we have no right to either. We don't know better than God if there is a problem with our righteousness! We can let it go.

Your forgiveness and justification in Jesus are complete. You have received His righteousness and do not appear to God anymore as a sinner. Paul said of Jesus, "[Y]et He has now reconciled you in His fleshly body through death, in order to present you before Him holy and blameless and beyond reproach" (Col. 1:22).

Before receiving these new truths of grace, when I would read the accounts of Jesus' life, I used to feel like he was condemning me every time he criticized one of the teachers of the law. But one day I saw that Jesus criticized only the self-righteous—those who thought they were super holy but really were not. He did not give the "sinners" a hard time about their sin. He hung out with the "sinners" and was criticized for doing so (Matt. 11:19). Jesus is not condemning you, just as He did not condemn the woman caught in adultery (John 8).

Do you believe that God is at peace with you? Paul says, "Therefore, having been justified by faith, we have peace with God through our Lord Jesus Christ" (Rom. 5:1). Having peace with God is described here as a result of justification by faith and nothing else. Note that it does NOT say "now that we have confessed all our sins, God is at peace with us" or "if we have lived a righteous life, God is at peace with us." Because you have received His righteousness as a gift, God is at peace with you now and forevermore! Many of us have a hard time believing that God is at peace with us because it's so rare for us to experience unconditional love on this fallen planet.

Before my life was transformed by grace, I found that whenever I sinned, I usually ran *from* His presence and not *to* Him. If He is a God who is upset with me for my sin, then why would I run to Him? But under grace He is at peace with us and desires for us to run *to* Him to find help when we sin. We can come boldly to His throne at any time because He wants to help us. The writer of Hebrews says, "Therefore let us draw near with confidence to the throne of grace, so that we may receive mercy and find grace to help in time of need" (Heb. 4:16). The phrase "grace to help" here is more the meaning of "supernatural help" because the other meaning of grace, which is "unmerited favor," does not fit as well in this context.

Not only can we run to Him after we sin, but we can run to Him when we are tempted, knowing that He has no condemnation for us. We can ask Him to help us not sin and to remove the temptation from us. Jesus said that we can pray "and lead us not into temptation" (Matt. 6:13). This is what grace gives us the confidence to do.

Holy of Holies

In the temple there was a curtain that separated the Holy place from the Holy of Holies room which contained the Ark of the Covenant and where the presence of God dwelt. In the Old Testament only the high priest could enter the Holy of Holies once a year.

When Jesus died, Matthew records, "And behold, the veil of the temple was torn in two from top to bottom" (Matt. 27:51). God tore the curtain at the death of Jesus to show us that our way to Him is fully open and has been fully paid for. You have full access to a forgiving, loving and accepting God. You can come into His presence with full assurance that He accepts you. The writer of Hebrews declares, "Therefore, brethren, since we have confidence to enter the holy place by the blood of Jesus, by a new and living way which He inaugurated for us through the veil, that is, His flesh, and since we have a great priest over the house of God, let us draw near with a sincere heart in full assurance of faith" (Heb. 10:19–22). He is inviting you in to have an unhindered relationship with Him all the time— not just once a year like the high priest was invited into the Holy of Holies.

The Light Burden

Do you think that God's expectations of you are a heavy burden? Jesus says, "Come to Me, all who are weary and heavy-laden, and I will give you rest. Take My yoke upon you and learn from Me, for I am gentle and humble in heart, and you will find rest for your souls. For My yoke is easy and My burden is light" (Matt. 11:28–30). His yoke is easy and his burden is light! This is what it's like to live under grace. He does not put the heavy weight of the law on you but rather removes it. Have you experienced the lightness of Jesus' burden?

Since it was not our good works that restored our fellowship with God in the first place, it is not our good works that keeps God happy with us. Paul says, "For by grace you have been saved through faith; and that not of yourselves, it is the gift of God; not as a result of works, so that no one may boast" (Eph. 2:8–9). It is entirely a gift that we just humbly receive, realizing that we were spiritually powerless to achieve it ourselves. This is why Jesus said that we must enter the Kingdom of Heaven like little children. He is talking about the humility of a child and that we need that kind of humility to receive such a large gift. Proud people have a hard time receiving anything because they want to be able to pay it back. It takes humility to receive something when we know we can't pay it back. We are at the mercy of the gift giver. It takes humility to receive Jesus' gift because we have to acknowledge that we were in a powerless state to get righteousness on our own.

Radical Grace

Hebrews chapter 10 is one of the most radical passages about grace in the Bible. This may be why I have never heard a sermon preached on it. The writer is comparing the imperfect Old Testament system of animal sacrifices for forgiveness to the perfect New Testament system of justification through faith in Jesus. Let's look at the first few verses.

For the Law, since it has only a shadow of the good things to come and not the very form of things, can never, by the same sacrifices which they offer continually year by year, make perfect those who draw near. Otherwise, would they not have ceased to be offered, because the worshipers, having once been cleansed, would no longer have had consciousness of sins? But in those sacrifices there is a reminder of sins year by year (Heb. 10:1–3).

The writer of Hebrews first talks about how the sacrifices offered were a shadow (literally "a sketch outline") of the ultimate sacrifice of Jesus for us. They were never the ultimate, perfect solution but pointed forward to what God would do on the cross.

Then he says that the old system cannot "make perfect those who draw near," implying that the new system *can* do this. Strong's *Exhaustive Concordance of the Bible* definition for the Greek word for "make perfect" as "to bring to an end, to complete, perfect." This is what Jesus did for us in forgiving us and giving us His righteousness.

The fact that they had to keep sacrificing every year is a sign that there was something deficient in the old system. If it had been a sufficient system, then they would have stopped making sacrifices year after year and, as the Hebrews passage says, the worshipers would "no longer have consciousness of sins." This implies that the new system *does* enable the worshiper to not have consciousness of sins. In the old system, the worshipers had repeated consciousness of sins, and thus the sacrifices were still offered every year. What does it mean to not "have consciousness of sin?" It means, at least, not having a constant reminder that we are sinners in general. It may also mean our not having a constant focus on our specific sins, which we will look at later in this chapter.

In the new system, there was one sacrifice given for all people for all time. The passage says that in the sacrifices were a "reminder of sins year by year." But Jesus was the one sacrifice for all time, so there is no longer a reminder of sin because sin was completely dealt with on the cross for all time.

This chapter also contains some other radical verses that I have previously quoted, such as the following:

17 "And their sins and their lawless deeds I will remember no more."

19 "Therefore, brethren, since we have confidence to enter the holy place by the blood of Jesus . . ."

22 "[L]et us draw near with a sincere heart in full assurance of faith, having our hearts sprinkled clean from an evil conscience and our bodies washed with pure water."

God *knows* that we are sinners and that eventually we will sin again. He doesn't expect us to be 100 percent sin-free. If we could fix ourselves in regard to sin, then Jesus' death would not have been necessary. God is not sitting around waiting for us to mess up again so that He can condemn us. It has all been dealt with on the cross. Even the Apostle Paul did not achieve a nearly sinless state. He confirms that he was not just a sinner but the *foremost* sinner (1 Tim. 1:15). He doesn't say that he used to be, but that he currently *is* the foremost sinner. Jesus didn't just forgive us of all our sins at the time of salvation—his blood continually cleanses us from all sin.

Hold on a Minute!

Someone might say, "If all you are saying about grace is true, then why don't we just sin all we want?" First of all, we know that the Apostle Paul taught radical grace because he anticipated this very question. He addresses and answers it in Romans 6, right after he spent chapters 1–3 talking about the sin of man and then in chapters 3–5 arguing for grace: "What shall we say then? Are we to continue in sin so that grace may increase? May it never be! How shall we who died to sin still live in it? Or do you not know that all of us who have been baptized into Christ Jesus have been baptized into His death?

Therefore we have been buried with Him through baptism into death, so that as Christ was raised from the dead through the glory of the Father, so we too might walk in newness of life" (Rom. 6:1–4).

Why would we want to continue in sin when it is sin that is hurting us or others around us? Sin is what is outside the will of God for us, and it is not in His perfect plan. It is a distortion and corruption of His original perfect creation. We can get deceived into thinking it is desirable and that God is keeping something good from us. We might think that we know better than God and that we can't trust Him.

This is what Adam and Eve thought in the Garden of Eden when they were told not to eat the forbidden fruit. "When the woman saw that the tree was good for food, and that it was a delight to the eyes, and that the tree was desirable to make one wise, she took from its fruit and ate; and she gave also to her husband with her, and he ate" (Gen. 3:6). Satan tries to convince us that God is holding out on something good for us. But sin causes untold destruction in our lives and in the lives of the people we affect with it. Why would we want that to continue?

Sin Is Not Our First Focus

If the continual focus of our lives is sin-avoidance, then Satan effectively keeps us from being used by God to minister to other people. This is an example of the good shutting out the best. Instead, God calls us to live by the Spirit and be in tune with what He is doing in and through us in His kingdom. Jesus is the King of a spiritual kingdom on the earth right now (Matt. 3:2; 6:33; 12:28), and He invites us to join Him in what He is doing.

Allow me to suggest a short experiment. Spend 15 seconds right now NOT thinking about the color blue.

Were you able to avoid thinking about the color blue? Most people can't. And the same difficulty exists if the focus of our life is sin. Thinking about it can actually empower sin in our lives. The only way to not focus on it is to have our focus on something else. In this case, if we have our focus on Jesus and what He is doing right now in His kingdom, then sin will not be on our minds.

When we are not preoccupied with sin, it loses its power. Paul says, "It was for freedom that Christ set us free; therefore keep standing firm and do not be subject again to a yoke of slavery" (Gal. 5:1). He is calling the law a yoke of slavery. But we are now free from the law and free in the Spirit. Paul talks again about the freedom we now have when he says, "Now the Lord is the Spirit, and where the Spirit of the Lord is, there is freedom" (2 Cor. 3:17 NIV). Focusing on what the Spirit is doing naturally keeps us from sin. Paul says again, "But I say, walk by the Spirit, and you will not carry out the desire of the flesh" (Gal. 5:16).

God wants us to put sin aside (repent) and get our focus on Jesus. We are especially encouraged to do this by the writer of Hebrews because there is a host of believers in heaven who are watching the race we are running and likely cheering us on. "Therefore, since we have so great a cloud of witnesses surrounding us, let us also lay aside every encumbrance and the sin which so easily entangles us, and let us run with endurance the race that is set before us, fixing our eyes on Jesus, the author and perfecter of faith" (Heb. 12:1–2). God calls us to keep the eyes of our heart continually on Jesus and what He is doing. I believe that this is one of the main keys to our spiritual success. Peter walked on the water as long as his eyes were on Jesus. When he took his eyes off Jesus, he started to sink. Paul also encourages us in our focus: "Therefore if you have been raised up with Christ, keep seeking the things above, where Christ is, seated at the right hand of God" (Col. 3:1).

Jesus tells us: "But seek first His kingdom and His righteousness, and all these things will be added to you" (Matt. 6:33). Here He affirms that our eyes should be focused on His kingdom. But what does it mean to also seek His righteousness? Many Bible commentators are unclear about exactly what this phrase means. Seeking His righteousness could be referring to seeking the righteousness that He gives us as a gift. Note that it does not say "seek first your own righteousness" but rather "His righteousness." The righteousness we are focusing on is God's since we are not righteous. W.E. Vine's *An Expository Dictionary of NT Words* says in this context that "righteousness" here means "the sum total of the requirements of God." But these are all met in us by Jesus. At the very least, it is about keeping our eyes on the righteousness of God. This is in contrast to focusing our lives on our sin. Focusing on the righteousness of God is in agreement with keeping our eyes first on Jesus. He is "the Righteous One" (1 John 2:1 NIV).

There is another important reason for sin to not be our primary focus, which we will find by looking again into the Garden of Eden story.

The Forbidden Fruit Syndrome

God told Adam and Eve that they could eat of any tree in the garden except for the tree of the knowledge of good and evil (Gen. 2:17). This is the tree they ended up eating from even though the garden probably contained countless other trees that also offered desirable fruit.

There is a psychological principle at work when something is forbidden: we tend to want it more. Tell a child what he specifically can't do, and what will he want to do? When something is forbidden or restricted, it makes it more enticing. We tend to think, "This must be something good I'm missing out on."

Having laws on what is prohibited in our lives can have the same effect. This is why the law was powerless to produce real change in people but instead produced more sin. Paul talks about this when he says, "I would not have known about coveting if the Law had not said, 'You shall not covet.' But sin, taking opportunity through the commandment, produced in me coveting of every kind; for apart from the Law sin is dead" (Rom. 7:7–9).

How Then Do We Live?

Paul addresses this question when he says, "All things are lawful for me, but not all things are profitable. All things are lawful for me, but I will not be mastered by anything" (1 Cor. 6:12) and "All things are lawful, but not all things edify" (1 Cor. 10:23).

He makes the radical grace statement that "all things are lawful." There are no more external rules with God. We are righteous and justified in the sight of God, and nothing (no rule breaking) can change that. Paul also says, "I know and am convinced in the Lord Jesus that nothing is unclean in itself" (Rom. 14:14). In the light of all things being lawful, he continues by giving us three general principles to live by:

1. Not all things are profitable

2. I will not be mastered by anything

3. Not all things edify

Sin is not profitable for us because it does not produce good fruit in our lives. It only produces destruction, not real benefits. Sin can also be master over us when we are living in defeat to it or have addictions. And if our sin affects other people negatively, then it certainly does not edify them (build them up and help them).

If we live under law, then the resulting condemnation can result in our feeling worse. This can drive us to sin to feel better, and then more condemnation results. This is a vicious cycle. Jesus offers to break us free from this cycle. Once we have experienced grace and are not living by a set of rules, then we are free in the Spirit to walk away from the things that are not profitable, master us or hurt other people.

Paul says that we have a new way of living in freedom from the external law when we are controlled by the inner dwelling of the Holy Spirit. He says, "Now the Lord is the Spirit, and where the Spirit of the Lord is, there is liberty" (2 Cor. 2:17). We can live a life in the Spirit that is free of condemnation and guilt trips. We are free to love God and others and let the Spirit empower us to be like Jesus. Under grace, we can run *to* God instead of *from* him.

Jesus affirmed that loving God and loving others was the whole point of the law in the first place. He said in Matthew 22:37 and 39 that the whole law can be summed up in two commands:

1. You shall love the Lord your God with all your heart, and with all your soul, and with all your mind.

2. You shall love your neighbor as yourself.

In the Old Testament, they only had the external law, which was powerless to produce internal change. In the New Testament era, we have the Holy Spirit who changes us from the inside out and gives us the heart and mind of Christ supernaturally. This is what happens when we are "born again" (John 3:3). The Spirit inside us gives us new life. Paul said, "I have been crucified with Christ; and it is no longer I who live, but Christ lives in me" (Gal. 2:20). He also added, "Therefore if anyone is in Christ, he is a new creature; the old things passed away; behold, new things have come" (2 Cor. 5:17).

We are not living under the external control of a written law anymore or by a set of rules; instead, we have a new life in the Spirit who empowers us and guides us. Paul says, "But now we have been released from the Law, having died to that by which we were bound, so that we serve in newness of the Spirit and not in oldness of the letter" (Rom. 7:6).

Forgiving Others

Once we receive the great forgiveness of God for our sins, it becomes much easier for us to forgive others. What God has forgiven us is immeasurably greater than any sin ever committed against us. Jesus made this clear in the parable of the unforgiving slave who did not forgive a fellow slave a small debt after the master had forgiven him a huge debt (Matt. 18:23–35).

Seeing Grace In The New Testament

As God revealed more to me about grace, I then started seeing grace all through the New Testament. It appeared in many passages that I had read before but that my eyes had not been opened to see the grace in. There are significant passages of grace in many places, including Romans 2–8, Galatians and Hebrews 8–10. These are definitely worth revisiting with grace glasses.

But how do we handle all the "do" statements that remain in the New Testament, the verses that tell us to take an active role in our faith? We can view these in the light of grace! They are not meant to be used as a new version of the law. We are not under the law anymore. Instead, they are to be taken as encouragement for godly living. Many times, these exhortations come only after a foundation of grace is established. For example, Paul details salvation and grace in Romans chapters 1-7 before he gives instruction for godly living in the rest of the book. He does the same in Galatians by laying a foundation of grace in chapters 1-4 before he gives suggestions for godly living in chapters 5-6. The New Testament is all about the love of God. He has something amazing for us in salvation and grace. He is cheering us on to live for Jesus as we head to the finish line.

CHAPTER SIX

Freedom in Ministry

After accepting these new truths about grace, I was set free and had great joy. I then asked God, "OK, what do I *do* now?" But the whole point of grace is that I was acceptable in His sight without *doing*, and He led me to do nothing specific for a year and a half. This was the ultimate test for me of my new beliefs about grace, because during this time I did no Christian service of any kind and trusted that God was pleased with me.

At the same time, I knew that I was still fundamentally burned out and that I had nothing in my flesh to offer God. I was holding on tight to the promise that apart from Him I could do nothing. I was determined to not go back to a life of spiritual obligation and working in the flesh. Before I moved forward in any ministry, I was looking to the Lord for internal empowerment in my spirit or an external clear direction. I knew that He had to supernaturally empower me for a ministry or otherwise I could not do it. It *had* to be clearly Him and not me.

Under grace we do not have to do Christian service to be righteous. We do it when the Holy Spirit empowers us to do it. To me, empowerment comes in the form of a desire, compassion or love for people. He lays burdens on my heart for specific ministries that are the burdens He also feels. The Holy Spirit energizes me to work in those areas, and He gives me His joy in it.

If I do ministry without His empowerment for long enough, then I know that spiritual burnout will result. Burnout happens when we give out of an empty tank. We give when we don't have the energy to give. We may even be empowered for a ministry, but if we give out more than God has given us to give, then it can also result in burnout. I wonder, if the Holy Spirit's presence were removed from churches today, how much church activity would still go on. Thankfully, I currently attend a church in which the power and leadership of the Holy Spirit is evident.

So, for a year and a half I waited on the Holy Spirit for direction and empowerment in ministry while I rejoiced in the grace and goodness of God.

The Disciples' Period of No Ministry

The disciples also had a period of time in which no ministry took place. They first learned how to do ministry by watching Jesus do ministry and then by going out in pairs themselves. Before they went out, Jesus "gave them power and authority over all the demons and to heal diseases" (Luke 9:1), and they flowed in that power.

But Jesus prophesied that there would be a "night" coming when they couldn't do ministry. He spoke of this when He was about to heal a man born blind and said, "We must work the works of Him who sent Me as long as it is day; night is coming when no one can work" (John 9:4). Bible commentators think that this "spiritual night" might refer to Jesus' death or our death, but they are not in agreement.

It seems reasonable to me that this "spiritual night" period of no work could have been the period of time between Jesus' crucifixion and the Day of Pentecost, when the Holy Spirit came. This includes the 40-day period between Jesus' resurrection and His ascension to heaven (Acts 1:3) and the extra time period of "not many days from now" (Acts 1:5) between the ascension and Pentecost.

During this total time of 40-plus days, there is no record of the disciples doing any ministry (thus the "spiritual night"). For at least the first eight days of that time, they were in hiding for fear of the Jews (John 20:19, 26). Then at some point in the middle of this period, Peter and some other disciples returned to their old business of fishing (John 21).

There were many encounters that the disciples had with Jesus during the 40 days. Not once did Jesus criticize them for not going out to do ministry. But He did criticize them for not believing what He had said in advance about His rising from the dead (Mark 16:14).

Later in the 40 days and then right before Jesus' ascension, He gave them two different instructions:

1. Go to all nations and make disciples (Matt. 28:19) and

2. Wait in the city until you receive power from the Holy Spirit (Luke 24:49).

He told them to leave and do ministry in all the world but first stay until they had received the Holy Spirit power. After the ascension, we know only that they were "continually in the temple" (Luke 24:53). Jesus apparently did not expect them to start doing ministry during the 40-plus days of the spiritual night, nor did He want them to.

The Disciples' Ministry Led by the Holy Spirit

Then after the Holy Spirit came on the Day of Pentecost, the disciples were spiritually set on fire, and 3,000 people were saved in the first day. The church expanded rapidly because of all the super-naturally empowered ministry that the disciples did.

The disciples were dependent on the Holy Spirit not only for empowerment for ministry, but also for leadership in ministry. I saw this leadership of the Holy Spirit when I read through the book of Acts for the first time in college. I was shocked to see that the ultimate leader of ministry was not one of the apostles but rather the Holy Spirit. I was surprised because I had never been taught in church that the Holy Spirit was the director of ministry, and I was not aware of any of the churches that I had attended up to that point operating in this manner. All ministries and programs had seemed to be a "good idea" that had been generated from man's wisdom.

Many times in the book of Acts we find the Holy Spirit giving directions to the disciples, telling then where He wanted them to go or not go, what they should do and whom they should talk to. Here are several examples:

8:29 "Then the Spirit said to Philip, 'Go up and join this chariot.'
10:19 "While Peter was reflecting on the vision, the Spirit said to him, 'Behold, three men are looking for you.'
11:12 "The Spirit told me to go with them without misgivings."
13:2 "[T]he Holy Spirit said, 'Set apart for Me Barnabas and Saul for the work to which I have called them.'"
16:6 "They passed through the Phrygian and Galatian region, having been forbidden by the Holy Spirit to speak the word in Asia[.]"

Yes, Peter did some leading of the church in Jerusalem in the early days of the church, but he was still led by the Holy Spirit. The disciples were eventually all scattered because of persecution, and the Holy Spirit continued leading them wherever they went.

We Also Wait on the Holy Spirit

This is the model for us to do ministry today. The Holy Spirit is given to us at the point of salvation, but the example of the 40-plus days is that God wants us to only do ministry that is led and empowered by the Holy Spirit. This is in clear contrast to us doing things we think we "should" do or that we think are a good idea. Whenever you find yourself using the word "should" in regard to ministry, or if you are doing something out of guilt or obligation, consider that you may have stepped back onto the performance treadmill of a subtle form of legalism. The Holy Spirit does not motivate us through guilt but through love and compassion. Paul said that if his works for God were not motivated by love, then it profited him nothing:

If I speak with the tongues of men and of angels, but do not have love, I have become a noisy gong or a clanging cymbal. If I have the gift of prophecy, and know all mysteries and all knowledge; and if I have all faith, so as to remove mountains, but do not have love, I am nothing. And if I give all my possessions to feed the poor, and if I surrender my body to be burned, but do not have love, it profits me nothing (1 Cor. 13:1–3).

Maybe you have heard it said that "God can't steer a parked car" or "Don't just stand there; do something!" This implies that you "should" just start doing anything, whether it is God's will or not, and He will correct your path along the way. But in the book of Acts the disciples were absolutely waiting on the Holy Spirit before they started reaching a lost world. They waited until they were "clothed with power from on high" (Luke 24:49) on the Day of Pentecost. Could 3,000 people have been saved through the disciples before the Holy Spirit came on them? No! They changed the world (Acts 17:6). This is what God wants to do in and through us!

This all ties into grace because we are not working in our own strength to be like Jesus and to do ministry. This is how Jesus' yoke is easy and His burden is light (Matt. 11:30). We have the freedom to relax and wait on Him. Generating Christian activity in our own strength does nothing to please Him.

Under grace you are free to do only the ministry led by and empowered by the Holy Spirit. Jesus said, "Abide in Me, and I in you. As the branch cannot bear fruit of itself unless it abides in the vine, so neither can you unless you abide in Me. I am the vine, you are the branches; he who abides in Me and I in him, he bears much fruit, for apart from Me you can do nothing" (John 15:4–5).

Before I learned about grace, the verse "apart from Me you can do nothing" used to offend me. Jesus was claiming that I was spiritually helpless on my own. I used to think, "Well, certainly I can do something for God on my own. I can pray or witness."

After I learned about grace, this verse gave me great comfort. It's telling me that I should not even try to do anything for God in my own strength because it will be futile. It is saying that apart from the power of Jesus in my life, I can't do anything for God's kingdom that will be significant or lasting. It won't produce any fruit or result in an eternal reward. This gives me the freedom to relax and follow the direction and empowerment of the Holy Spirit.

We are like the small branches of a grape plant that are attached to the thick vine. The small branches produce the grapes, but of course all the water and nutrients come to it through the thick vine. If a small branch were cut off from the vine, it would be capable of producing nothing but would shrivel up. That is how helpless we are to produce the fruit of the Spirit without being connected to the living vine.

John the Baptist

John the Baptist was a rare person who was filled with the Holy Spirit before he was born (Luke 1:15). He is a great example of someone who had true humility and knew that he was not accomplishing anything for God in himself.

But Jesus said that John was great: "Truly I say to you, among those born of women there has not arisen anyone greater than John the Baptist!" (Matt. 11:11).

John's humility was one of the things that made him great. As an example of this, some people came to him during the later days of his ministry and told him that everyone was now going to Jesus (or rather to Jesus' disciples) to get baptized. John's response is stunning: "A man can receive nothing unless it has been given him from heaven" (John 3:27). He recognized that all the ministry he was doing was entirely directed and empowered by God. There was nothing of himself. When his ministry was declining, he knew there was nothing he could do about it because he was not responsible for it in the first place. John said of Jesus, "He must increase, but I must decrease" (John 3:30). This is also an amazing statement and a model for us in the ministries that God calls us to. Jesus must increase in visibility and glory, and we must decrease. The glory must all go to Him, for He does everything through us.

Jesus Did Only What the Father Was Doing

The way the disciples were led and empowered by the Holy Spirit in Acts is similar to how Jesus was empowered by the Holy Spirit and did only the ministry that the Father showed Him to do. The Holy Spirit descended on Jesus at his baptism (Luke 3:21-22) and

He "returned to Galilee in the power of the Spirit" (Luke 4:14). Jesus said, "Truly, truly, I say to you, the Son can do nothing of Himself, unless it is something He sees the Father doing; for whatever the Father does, these things the Son also does in like manner" (John 5:19). He also said only what the Father gave him to say: "For I did not speak on My own initiative, but the Father Himself who sent Me has given Me a commandment as to what to say and what to speak" (John 12:49).

Jesus' life is the ultimate model of Christian ministry because He was the only perfect one. He showed that in ministry he was led by the Father. Jesus said, "For I have come down from heaven, not to do My own will, but the will of Him who sent Me" (John 6:38).

Jesus healed only one man at the pool at Bethesda (John 5) even though there were many other disabled people there. When Jesus was there and saw all the sick people, He could have thought, "The right thing for me to do here is to heal all these people" or "I 'should' heal all these people in need. How irresponsible or uncaring would I be if I didn't?" But He didn't. For any of us, this would have been a great opportunity to experience a guilt trip. But He only did what the Father led Him to do, which was to heal one person. We don't know why the Father only led Him to heal one person. We only know that, likewise, God wants us to only do what He leads us to do.

At the start of Jesus' ministry, He had performed some miracles in Capernaum, and then He went to his hometown Nazareth and read from Isaiah in the synagogue. The people wanted Him to perform miracles there, but He did not because, He said, "[N]o prophet is welcome in his hometown" (Luke 4:24). The people were angry at Him for this. He answered by explaining that God performed only selective miracles at two different times in the Old Testament even when there were many other people in urgent need. He mentioned Elijah who supernaturally made the oil and flour not run out for one widow he stayed with when there were many other widows present during the famine. He also mentioned one leper who was healed by Elisha when there were many other lepers present.

Jesus was following exactly what the Father was leading Him to do or not do in that situation. He trusted the Father's leading and did not come up with a ministry plan himself for what seemed right at the time, even when there were many other apparently urgent needs.

Not Doing the Urgent

Likewise, God calls us to trust Him for ministry plans and for His leadership. Just because we see an urgent need in the church does not mean that God desires for us to be the one to fill it. He wants us to trust in His sovereign plan and not take ministry decisions into our own hands. There may be many great ministry opportunities presented to us in our church that we might think we "should" do. But God wants us to do only the things that He is leading us to do.

It is not enough that someone whom we respect in church leadership asks us to participate in a ministry. We need to ask God to confirm that He wants us to do it. We can pray and ask God to bring us and the leadership to one mind regarding what we are to participate in. If He is not empowering us for the ministry, then we would be doing it in our flesh and it won't produce fruit or count for eternity.

Conclusion

If Jesus did and said only what the Father gave Him to do and say, and if the apostles needed the Holy Spirit to lead and empower them in ministry, then we certainly need to do likewise. The Holy Spirit is still the leader of ministry today. He is supernaturally leading countless people in the church and in the mission fields.

If you are on the performance treadmill of duty and obligation, then it is time to get off! These are subtle forms of legalism and only result in burnout.

CHAPTER SEVEN

Power in Ministry

After I had waited on the Holy Spirit for a year and a half to show me how He wanted to use me in the kingdom, the power and presence of the Holy Spirit unexpectedly came on me and others at my church on Sunday, March 6, 1994.

My pastor gave a message and spoke of a movement of God happening in various places. At the end of his message, he invited people to come forward to receive prayer if they felt like this movement of God had begun in them. I felt nothing. I did not go forward and instead ended up leaving to go home. But I had a strange feeling that church wasn't done yet. When I walked into my home, the presence of the Holy Spirit came on me in great power and in a way that I had never experienced before. I was immediately driven to my knees to pray for the salvation of three coworkers at my job. The compassion of the Lord was upon me for these men, and I was weeping and grieving over their eternal destination.

This was *clearly* not from me. I had been working with these men for the better part of eight years. Never once had I prayed for their salvation. Never once had I witnessed to them. Never once had I experienced compassion for their eternal destination. But now here I was on my knees, uncontrollably weeping for them and asking God to reach out to them and save them.

This was the first of many new God encounters that happened over the next two weeks and have continued to this day, 25 years later. On that first day, the Holy Spirit gave me the new gift of intercession, among other things. It was powerful and life-changing. In a radical change from my previous dead prayer life, I now experienced strongly the compassion and presence of God when praying for people. I saw God work in people's lives as I had never seen before. Up until that time, as I previously mentioned, prayer meetings had been incredibly boring to me and I had tried to avoid them. This new work in me was clearly not me but God in me!

Before this happened, I could recall only a few times where I saw God supernaturally intervening in my life. After this happened, I started keeping track of every "God thing" that I saw Him do, including every time that His presence came on me supernaturally to pray. I have recorded in that journal for 25 years, and it is currently 180 pages long. I experience His presence and power so often now that I have stopped recording most things that happen. This is all the Lord's doing.

Power Perfected in Weakness

The Apostle Paul says God told him, "My grace is sufficient for you, for power is perfected in weakness," and then Paul continues, "Most gladly, therefore, I will rather boast about my weaknesses, so that the power of Christ may dwell in me" (2 Cor. 12:9). This was my experience. The more I accepted the fact that in my flesh I have spiritually nothing to offer and admitted it to others, the greater the power of God I saw on my life.

Our brokenness is a door for God's power. This seems like a strange principle, but God says that "He gives grace to the humble." God wants to show His power in the middle of our weakness so that it is obvious that it is all Him. He wants to take all the credit for what He does through us. God says, "I am the Lord, that is My name;

I will not give My glory to another" (Isaiah 42:8). He wants us to recognize that we have nothing in ourselves that is useful for His kingdom. His power and glory working through us is in stark contrast to the weakness of our flesh. When we are weak, then we can't take credit for anything He does through us because it is so obvious that it wasn't us.

Paul says, "Such confidence we have through Christ toward God. Not that we are adequate in ourselves to consider anything as coming from ourselves, but our adequacy is from God" (2 Cor. 3:4–5). He also says, "[F]or it is God who is at work in you, both to will and to work for His good pleasure" (Phil. 2:13). God gives us both His desire to do ministry and the empowerment for it. Nothing is of us. The more we accept this, the more He can supernaturally use us.

I have repeatedly seen this principle at work in a few, very anointed ministers. These are people through whom the power and presence of God repeatedly manifests. They have a complete humility and understanding that they have nothing spiritual in themselves. They continually talk about how they are not spiritual and even give examples of it. But I assure you that the power of God rests on them.

Waiting on God's Power

There is great power that we can experience when we wait on God and ask Him to empower us. But we must be patient and not rush into a ministry before He leads us. God tells us, "Be still, and know that I am God" (Psalm 46:10 NIV). He leads each one of us in different ways. But one relatively common way I see Him leading people is that He places His burdens on our hearts. When we find that we have a burden and special compassion for a certain group of people and it is obvious to us that it is not from our own strength, this may be a sign that He is leading us into ministry in that area. We can ask Him to give us compassion for those He has compassion for.

Matthew reports of Jesus, "When He went ashore, He saw a large crowd, and felt compassion for them and healed their sick" (Matt. 14:14). He did not heal them just to prove that He was God's son. He healed them because He had compassion on them. His compassion in us drives the ministry. God gives us His compassion for certain individuals or groups so that we know the direction in which to minister. Then He gives us Holy Spirit power to love with.

When we are talking to believers or nonbelievers, we can simply and silently ask God, "What is your heart for this person, and what are you wanting to do in their life?" This is an example of His yoke being easy. We don't have to figure out how to do ministry. We just need to wait in peace for Him to show His plan to us and to show us what His heart is for them. The Holy Spirit is our teacher. Perhaps He will give us words to say to a person or show us how to pray for them or help them in some other way.

Every morning we can wake up and ask Him, "What are You doing today in Your kingdom, and how can I be a part of it?" Jesus said, "My Father is working until now" (John 5:17). He is still working today and invites us to come alongside Him with what He is doing and to ask Him how we can be a part of it. He is the leader of ministry, not us. This is *His* kingdom.

We don't need to invent new programs or ministries in the church based on our own spiritual wisdom and brilliant ideas. God always has a plan. We don't need to pressure people in the church to be more involved in ministries. We can pray and trust that the Holy

Spirit has a plan, and we can pray in agreement with what He wants to do and who He wants to lead and empower for ministry.

Every believer has the Holy Spirit living inside them from the day of salvation (Rom. 8:9). But each person has various spiritual gifts and in different measures. In particular, Paul says, "God has allotted to each a measure of faith" (Rom. 12:3). This implies that the exact same measure of faith is not given to everyone. Also, we certainly all know people who have much different and stronger gifts than we do. The Holy Spirit has given various gifts to believers and in different measures.

Asking for More of the Holy Spirit

There are different views on when the baptism of the Holy Spirit occurs in a believer's life, and I don't intend to argue one way or the other here. But whether it occurs at the time of salvation or is a later event, it is OK to ask for more of the power of the Holy Spirit in our lives. Jesus tells us to ask:

So I say to you, ask, and it will be given to you; seek, and you will find; knock, and it will be opened to you. For everyone who asks, receives; and he who seeks, finds; and to him who knocks, it will be opened. Now suppose one of you fathers is asked by his son for a fish; he will not give him a snake instead of a fish, will he? Or if he is asked for an egg, he will not give him a scorpion, will he? If you then, being evil, know how to give good gifts to your children, *how much more will your heavenly Father give the Holy Spirit to those who ask Him*? (Luke 11:9–13, emphasis mine).

I don't believe that this is a salvation verse because, in the context, Jesus is describing how we should persist in prayer because the Father wants to give us good gifts.

It's permissible for you to ask the Father for more of the presence and power of the Holy Spirit in your life. The verse above says that because He is a good father, He *wants* to give you more of the Holy Spirit! Ask and wait for Him to empower you for the ministries He wants you to do. There is no law or obligation here. There is only freedom, love and power in the Spirit.

Paul said that we should "earnestly desire the greater gifts" (1 Cor. 12:31). We can pray to ask God for more. He may give you new ministry burdens or gifts. This may happen when you are sitting at home alone. But I have seen that often He does a significant work in our lives when we go to a place where His Spirit is powerfully moving.

In terms of receiving healing, this was true of countless people whom Jesus healed. How many of them would have been healed if they had stayed at home and asked God for a healing? We mostly have accounts of people receiving healing because they pressed in to Jesus where the power of God was flowing. Of course, the centurion's servant was healed without Jesus physically being there, but the centurion came to Jesus to ask for it (Matt. 8:5–13).

Likewise, in Acts there are accounts of people receiving the power of the Holy Spirit in their lives when they were prayed for by an apostle who was anointed of God.

My point is, if you want to see more gifts and power of the Holy Spirit in your life, persistently ask God for it and wait on Him. But also consider finding people, churches or special events where the power of God is manifestly flowing and seek to receive from Him there. If you know a believer who strongly moves in the gifts, then ask him to pray for you to receive more.

If I had not been present at my church in 1994 when the power of God flowed, I don't believe that I would have received new spiritual gifts that day. It was the people who were present during the service who received from the Lord. My life has been irrevocably changed since that day.

When I experience the power of the Holy Spirit flowing through me to bless others, I want to continue pursuing these opportunities to be used by God out of the joy that He gives me and to experience His presence and power. Paul said, "For God has not given us a spirit of timidity, but of power and love and discipline" (2 Tim. 1:7). We don't work at this in our flesh. All we have to do is let the wind of the Holy Spirit blow through us.

This is in stark contrast to doing ministry out of an empty tank with an obligation that I must serve in order to be accepted by Him. We are already accepted in Jesus, which Paul confirms with this phrase: "to the praise of the glory of His grace, by which He made us accepted in the Beloved" (Eph.1:6 NKJV).

CHAPTER EIGHT

What about the Judgment of the Believer and Eternal Rewards?

The judgment of the believer after death is a critical issue to be addressed in the light of grace. The main question to be resolved is, If all of this is true about grace, and all of our sins are forgiven and we have His righteousness, then how can the believer come under judgment after death?

First, there is a difference between the judgment of the non-believer and that of the believer. The judgment of the nonbeliever is the great white throne judgment and ends in a decision of eternal separation from God for them because of their sins that have not been forgiven (Rev. 20:11–15). The judgment of the believer is for the purpose of determining rewards in heaven and is based on how we have lived our lives and on service to Jesus. Paul said, "For we must all appear before the judgment seat of Christ, so that each one may be recompensed for his deeds in the body, according to what he has done, whether good or bad" (2 Cor. 5:10). He also said, "So then each one of us will give an account of himself to God" (Rom. 14:12).

Second, I would like to address the more specific questions of 1) Why are there rewards in Heaven? 2) How much are they really worth since we are in heaven anyway? and 3) How does what we do now affect our rewards? An exhaustive study on rewards is beyond the scope of this book, but these are questions worth addressing in a general way to see how they relate to grace. We will look at one main parable of Jesus where he describes the judgment and rewards in the Kingdom of Heaven, and then we will look at some other scriptures.

Jesus as King

Jesus has many roles and associated titles. Just a few of His titles are the Lamb of God (John 1:29), the Lion of Judah (Rev. 5:5), the Righteous Judge (2 Tim. 4:8) and the King of Kings (Rev. 17:14). Paul says, "God highly exalted Him, and bestowed on Him the name which is above every name" (Phil. 2:9). His character has so many aspects that we will spend eternity getting to know Him better. When He was on earth, He showed at different times all of these characteristics. But while on earth He mainly came as the Lamb of God. When He comes the second time, He will still be the Lamb of God, but He will manifest as the King of Kings and then at the judgment as the Righteous Judge.

It is important to recognize that in heaven Jesus is a king of a real kingdom. In modern times, few people live in kingdoms, so this concept of living in a kingdom may be foreign to us. But most people throughout history have lived in kingdoms. The immediate listeners of Jesus' parables lived in a kingdom and might have related more easily to His parables of the Kingdom of Heaven than we can today.

An Old Kingdom

Let's look for a minute at the characteristics of an old kingdom before we look at one of Jesus' parables of the Kingdom of Heaven so that we may gain some insight. I would like to use the example of a medieval kingdom, even though it did not exist at the time of Jesus, because we can relate to it better since it is closer to our time.

In a medieval kingdom, there is a king who has absolute authority and rule. He has immediate and extended family members who are royalty. His sons and daughters are princes and princesses, and he has many nobles who rule over territories of his kingdom. Different nobles have various levels of responsibility and authority. There are knights who fight for the king, and there is an army. There are people with specific skills such as blacksmiths, fabric makers, merchants and traders and so on. And there are many peasants who work the fields and husband the animals. In a kingdom, the king desires good servants. He can seek and reward good servants. He has absolute authority and can reward any person as he judges. Regardless of their rewards, all his subjects are members of the kingdom.

Jesus' Kingdom

Likewise, Jesus is the King of Kings and Lord of Lords of a real kingdom. We cannot imagine at this time the glory, majesty and power that we will see in Him in heaven. I believe that when we see Him, we will see clearly that there was no greater purpose for our lives on earth than to serve Him. Everything else pales in comparison. All authority in heaven and earth has been given to Him (Matt. 28:18), and one day every knee will bow and tongue will confess in heaven and on earth and in hell that He is Lord over everything (Phil. 2:10–11).

It is worth noting that our positions and rewards in heaven span a wide range. Jesus talked often in the parables of the kingdom about how the ruler had good to bad servants and how they received significantly different levels of rewards, including various levels of ruling. Likewise, in a medieval kingdom there is a large difference between a noble and a peasant. But they are both still members and subjects of the kingdom.

Parable of the Kingdom

In the past I found that many of the parables of Jesus were difficult to understand, especially when trying to figure out who in the parables represents those who are saved versus not saved. I have rarely heard pastors try to interpret some of these parables.

But the parable of the minas (money) in Luke 19:11–27 sheds light on the Kingdom of Heaven and is key to understanding many other difficult parables. This parable is very similar to other parables of the kingdom (Matt. 25:14–30), but this one has a distinction in that an extra people group is represented (the enemies of the King). Luke strategically places this parable just before the Triumphal Entry, and just after the salvation of Zacchaeus.

11 While they were listening to this, he went on to tell them a parable, because he was near Jerusalem and the people thought that the kingdom of God was going to appear at once. 12 He said: "A man of noble birth went to a distant country to have himself appointed king and then to return. 13 So he called ten of his servants and gave them ten minas. 'Put this money to work,' he said, 'until I come back.' 14 "But his subjects hated him and sent a delegation after him to say, 'We don't want this man to be our king.' 15 "He was made king, however, and returned home. Then he sent for the servants to whom he had given the money, in order to find out what they had gained with it. 16 "The first one came and said, 'Sir, your mina has earned ten more.' 17 "'Well done, my good servant!' his master replied. 'Because you have been trustworthy in a very small matter, take charge of ten cities.' 18 "The second came and said, 'Sir, your mina has earned five more.' 19 "His master answered, 'You take charge

of five cities.' 20 "Then another servant came and said, 'Sir, here is your mina; I have kept it laid away in a piece of cloth. 21 I was afraid of you, because you are a hard man. You take out what you did not put in and reap what you did not sow.' 22 "His master replied, 'I will judge you by your own words, you wicked servant! You knew, did you, that I am a hard man, taking out what I did not put in, and reaping what I did not sow? 23 Why then didn't you put my money on deposit, so that when I came back, I could have collected it with interest?' 24 "Then he said to those standing by, 'Take his mina away from him and give it to the one who has ten minas.' 25 "'Sir,' they said, 'he already has ten!' 26 "He replied, 'I tell you that to everyone who has, more will be given, but as for the one who has nothing, even what they have will be taken away. 27 But those enemies of mine who did not want me to be king over them—bring them here and kill them in front of me.'" (Luke 19:11–27 NIV)

The nobleman who went off to be appointed king and then to return represents Jesus who will return a second time as King of Kings (Rev. 19:16). The subjects of the nobleman are citizens who hated him and did not want him to rule over them (v. 14). They are also called enemies of the nobleman (v. 27). These are unsaved people who reject Jesus as King and Savior.

This leaves the three servants of the nobleman representing saved people who serve Jesus as King. Note that there is a large difference between the servants and the subjects. The servants were apparently servants by choice, whereas the subjects hated the king and did not want him to rule over them. The subjects in the end were killed in front of the king, but none of the servants were, and they apparently remained as servants. These large differences suggest that the servants represent saved people and the subjects represent unsaved people.

Each servant was given money to invest while the master was gone, representing the gifts of the Spirit each believer is given. Each was to invest the gift and see it multiply. Jesus wants our seed of the kingdom that is within us (Luke 17:21) to multiply and produce much fruit (John 15:5). This is what the servants were tasked to do.

There Is a Huge Difference in Rewards

One servant multiplied the money he was entrusted with ten times, and the second servant multiplied it five times. These servants were commended by the king for being good servants and were given authority over ten and five cities, respectively (Luke 19:17–19). This was a huge reward for being faithful in a relatively small thing. This means that the rewards we are to receive in heaven have value far beyond the service we give on earth. A small amount of faithfulness will result in a great reward. The ruling of the cities is like a nobleman in our medieval kingdom who is given responsibility and authority over a territory.

However, the third servant did not multiply the money or even put it on deposit to earn interest. He received no reward. His mina was given to the servant with ten minas, and he was not given any cities to rule. He had been entrusted with the riches of the master but had done nothing with it. Jesus said, "From everyone who has been given much, much will be required" (Luke 12:48). The third servant's servanthood was evaluated as wicked (NASB says "worthless") by the master because the servant had done nothing for him when he had been entrusted with treasure to invest. As we saw earlier, this servant represents a saved person because he was a servant of the king and was not in the group of people who rejected the king's rule and were sentenced to death.

The difference in reward levels between the first servant and the third is staggering. Jesus is suggesting that this kind of difference exists in heaven between the highest level of reward and the lowest level of reward; otherwise, He would not have made this difference such a significant part of this parable. This is like the difference in our medieval kingdom between a noble and a peasant. Jesus is doing us a huge favor by telling us in advance of the different reward levels in heaven. Jesus said, "Look, I am coming soon! My reward is with me, and I will give to each person according to what they have done" (Rev. 22:12).

But even being in the lowest level of heaven is far greater than we can even imagine. In heaven, we will all have a glorious, imperishable body (1 Cor. 15:42–43). Jesus is the image of the invisible God (Col. 1:15), and when He comes back a second time we will be like Him. John said, "Beloved, now we are children of God, and it has not appeared as yet what we will be. We know that when He appears, we will be like Him, because we will see Him just as He is" (I John 3:2).

Service to the King

Note that in this parable the reward for a believer is based on his service to the master by multiplying the kingdom, not by whether he has sinned. Once again, this is not something we do in our own strength. Instead, we let the Holy Spirit multiply the kingdom through us by using the spiritual gifts He gives us. In heaven, our sins are absolutely all forgiven and Jesus has no righteous anger at us, but our service to King Jesus is still evaluated for rewards.

Servanthood is a key to kingdom rewards, as seen where Jesus said, "[B]ut whoever wishes to become great among you shall be your servant" (Mark 10:43). Servanthood is about being like Jesus. Jesus said of himself that "the Son of Man did not come to be served, but to serve, and to give His life a ransom for many" (Matt. 20:28).

God wants us to pursue the rewards in heaven; otherwise, He would not have given us so many parables telling us of rewards. It's not selfish to pursue eternal rewards. If you desire to be a good employee at your company so that you get a good raise next year, how much more should you desire to serve Jesus faithfully for the hope of eternal rewards?

The Highest Levels of Rewards Involve Ruling

A significant part of the mina parable focuses on the reward of ruling and authority. What is the analogy to this in the Kingdom of Heaven for the servants of Jesus who are found faithful in producing the fruit of the kingdom (Matt. 21:43)? Maybe Jesus used the example of ruling over ten cities to simply represent a "large reward." Maybe there is no ruling at all in the highest level of reward in heaven. But there are a few other clues in the Bible that suggest that ruling may be a part of the higher levels.

First, why would Jesus use the example of ruling to represent a large reward when He could have just said that the first servant received 100 minas as a reward? Maybe it is only because in a kingdom at the time this is how a king would reward his most trusted servants.

Paul gives us another clue about the possibility of ruling where he says, "If we endure, we will also reign with Him" (2 Tim. 2:12). Faithful believers are given the highest reward of reigning with Jesus. I don't believe this is a salvation verse because if it were, it would mean that a person would have to "endure" in order to be saved. The ruling reward is conditional on "if we endure." We know that salvation is not based on works but on faith in Jesus. "Enduring" would mean being faithful to continue serving Jesus throughout one's life and not falling away and serving one's own interests.

If some believers rule in heaven, then what are they ruling? Revelations describes the New Jerusalem which comes out of heaven and shines with the glory of God (Rev. 21:11). A few verses later we see that "[t]he nations will walk by its light, and the kings of the earth will bring their splendor into it" (Rev. 21:24). This implies that there will continue to be nations that exist outside of heaven. Believers in heaven may exercise some form of spiritual rule over the nations.

Also, we find that an Old Testament prophecy about Jesus indicates that His kingdom will continue to expand forever. This implies that people will continue to multiply. Isaiah 9:7 says of Jesus, "There will be no end to the increase of His government or of peace, On the throne of David and over his kingdom, To establish it and to uphold it with justice and righteousness From then on and forevermore."

A final piece comes from Revelations 22:5, which states that the inhabitants of the New Jerusalem that comes down from heaven "will reign forever and ever."

With this many references in the Bible to believers having a role of reigning in heaven, it would be reasonable to conclude that when Jesus spoke in His mina parable about the first and second servants receiving rewards of ruling over cities, it was not just a general example of a "large reward" but an indication that there is an element of real reigning in heaven at the higher levels of reward. It also implies that there is a huge difference in highest to lowest levels of rewards in heaven in the order of 10 to 1 or perhaps 100 to 1. What is the difference between the first servant getting ten cities to rule over and the third servant having his one mina taken away from him?

The Lowest Levels of Rewards Involve Initial Great Grief

How much grief did the third servant experience when the master judged him? The parable does not give us this information, but we can only imagine what we would have felt if we had been in his position.

First Corinthians 3:11–15 gives a picture of our work on earth for the Master and how it will be judged:

> For no one can lay any foundation other than the one already laid, which is Jesus Christ. If anyone builds on this foundation using gold, silver, costly stones, wood, hay or straw, their work will be shown for what it is, because the Day will bring it to light. It will be revealed with fire, and the fire will test the quality of each person's work. If what has been built survives, the builder will receive a reward. If it is burned up, the builder will suffer loss but yet will be saved— even though only as one escaping through the flames.

This is talking about our work and service for Jesus on earth, and "the Day will bring it to light" refers to the judgment of the believer. There will be a "fire" that will test what we have done on earth. Good-quality work will survive the fire, but bad-quality work of wood, hay or straw will be burned up and shown as useless and ineffective. The "builder will suffer loss" is referring to the grief the believer experiences when they realize that their life was wasted instead of using it to serve Jesus. What they did had no lasting eternal value.

Maybe they lived for themselves and for treasure on earth rather than living for Jesus and treasure in heaven. Jesus said, "Do not store up for yourselves treasures on earth, where moth and rust destroy, and where thieves break in and steal. But store up for yourselves treasures in heaven, where neither moth nor rust destroys, and where thieves do not break in or steal" (Matt. 6:19–20).

How much grief would we experience if our whole life were to be evaluated as hay, wood or straw (being worthless), and then burned up in the fire of judgment? The passage above says that we would "suffer loss." This would not be a pain-free experience, and we should not underestimate the devastation of that experience.

But it is *after* the judgment of the believer and when the new heaven and earth are revealed that every tear will be wiped away (Rev. 21:4). We will be in the glorious kingdom even though we will have different levels of eternal reward and rule.

The Parable of the Houses

Another key to eternal rewards can be found in Jesus' Sermon on the Mount in Matthew 5–7. He lays out many principles for godly living, which is all about being like Jesus. At the end, He gives this significant warning about following what He said:

Therefore everyone who hears these words of mine
and puts them into practice is like a wise man who built his

house on the rock. The rain came down, the streams rose, and the winds blew and beat against that house; yet it did not fall, because it had its foundation on the rock. But everyone who hears these words of mine and does not put them into practice is like a foolish man who built his house on sand. The rain came down, the streams rose, and the winds blew and beat against that house, and it fell with a great crash (Matt. 7:24–27).

It is often believed that the house built on the sand which was destroyed by the water refers to a person who is not saved and the house crashing is a picture of that person's being sentenced to hell. But Jesus does not make it clear if the house crashing on the sand represents a destination of hell.

On the other hand, this picture of the house crashing is consistent with the passage of an unfaithful believer's life consisting of hay, wood or straw being burned in the fire of judgment (1 Cor. 3:15) and also of the third servant whose mina was taken from him (Luke 19:24). In the case of a person's life of wood, hay or straw burning up, their life is shown to be useless and easily destroyed, much like the house on the sand is destroyed. Everything they built in their life came to nothing because it was all for them and not for Jesus. In the case of the minas, the third servant lost his only mina because of a life shown to be useless, also like the house crashing on the sand.

A commonly accepted principle of Bible interpretation is that when you encounter a passage that is not entirely clear in its meaning, you should find another passage on the same topic whose meaning is clearer and use the clearer passage to interpret the unclear passage. So, is Jesus talking about the method of salvation or of eternal rewards in this parable of the houses?

This parable is the conclusion to a long teaching on moral living, in which Jesus says that if you follow His moral teachings, then your life will be like the house on the rock; otherwise, it will be like the house on the sand. If this passage is about salvation, then His point would be that salvation is obtained through works. But we have already seen in many clear passages in chapter 1 that salvation is only through faith in Jesus and not through works. Therefore, we should use the clear passages on the method of salvation to interpret that this unclear passage of the house crashing is not talking about salvation but rather eternal rewards.

In many parables of Jesus, I used to assume that He was talking about salvation. But He was often speaking to many people who were His followers and believed in Him. It would be reasonable for him to also teach them about rewards in the kingdom.

The house being destroyed that was built on the sand is an image of the judgment of the believer who did not follow Jesus' godly life principles. At the judgment, his life was correctly seen as a waste, and it fell like a house of cards. But in this parable, eternal rewards were based on godly living rather than the believer multiplying the kingdom as in the parable of the minas.

Repentance (turning away from sin) is good because it makes us more like Jesus and increases our eternal reward. Our rewards are greater in heaven for serving Jesus and being like Him. The more we are like him, the more we are sin-free. This is why repentance has a positive effect on eternal rewards. John said, "Now, little children, abide in Him, so that when He appears, we may have confidence and not shrink away from Him in shame at His coming" (John 2:28). It is possible for our sins to be completely forgiven while our Christlikeness is still evaluated for rewards.

Another way to be like Jesus is in His humility. In Matthew 11:29, Jesus opened the curtains to His true inner self when He said, "[F]or I am gentle and humble in heart, and you will find rest for your souls."

Denying Ourselves and Living for Jesus

Another key to eternal rewards is found in Luke 9:23–24, where Jesus says, "If anyone wishes to come after Me, he must deny himself, and take up his cross daily and follow Me. For whoever wishes to save his life will lose it, but whoever loses his life for My sake, he is the one who will save it."

What does it mean that someone might "lose his life?" Again, this sounds like it could be talking about someone destined for hell. But there is a possibility that it refers to the same type of person whose life of hay, wood or straw is burned up in the fire of judgment but who is saved "yet so as through fire" (1 Cor. 3:15).

The question here for this passage is whether He is talking about salvation or rewards in heaven for the believer. If this passage is talking about the requirements for salvation, then the requirement to "deny himself, and take up his cross daily" would mean that salvation is again obtained through works. This would negate the clear passages that salvation is only through faith.

The description of someone in the end "losing his life" is consistent with the other images of the hay, wood or straw of a person's life being burned up at the judgment and of the house on the sand crashing.

Jesus calls us to deny ourselves, our own desires and pursuits, and live for Him and for His kingdom. He had large groups of people following Him (who likely generally believed in Him), and when He said, "if any wishes to come after me," He was making it clear to them what the cost of actual discipleship was (becoming more like Jesus), which would result in their lives having value for eternity. Their lives "being saved" refers to their lives being evaluated at the judgment as having been worthwhile for the King.

Everything Will Be Disclosed.

Adam and Eve went into hiding after they sinned (Gen. 3:8), and in Heaven, all hiding will end and everything will be disclosed. Paul says, "Therefore do not go on passing judgment before the time, but wait until the Lord comes who will both bring to light the things hidden in the darkness and disclose the motives of men's hearts; and then each man's praise will come to him from God" (1 Cor. 4:5). And Jesus said, "Accordingly, whatever you have said in the dark will be heard in the light, and what you have whispered in the inner rooms will be proclaimed upon the housetops" (Luke 12:3).

We Are Not Qualified to Judge Others' Rewards

The 1 Corinthians 4:5 passage above tells us to not judge one another because we don't know the motives of men's hearts and we don't know everything that is hidden. We are not called to be spiritual fruit inspectors for other believers. We don't know what measure of love, faith and spiritual gifts God has given them, so we don't know if they are using all of what they have received. We can live only for an audience of One. How other people are doing and how much fruit they are producing compared to us is meaningless to determine our eternal rewards.

Seeing Grace in Parables

Having an understanding that there is a large difference in high to low reward levels in heaven and that the low levels involve great grief at the judgment, showing our life to be worthless, helps us to interpret many passages in a new grace way that we would otherwise have difficulty interpreting. Without this understanding, we would be left with many passages that sound very anti-grace or that seem to claim that works is the method of salvation, which is also anti-grace.

Hold on Again Here!

The judgment of the believer still sounds contradictory to grace! How can Jesus give us His righteousness and still judge us for eternal rewards? Since we all have an equal and complete amount of the righteousness of Christ, if He were to grant rewards to us based purely on that righteousness, then we would all receive the exact same reward in Heaven. But the parables are very clear that there is a very large range of rewards in Heaven.

So, instead, He is using criteria for rewards based on service (expanding the kingdom) and being like Jesus. The parable of the minas speaks to expanding the kingdom while the parable of the two houses in the Sermon on the Mount speaks to being like Jesus. Being more like Jesus inherently means being more sin-free since He was absolutely sin-free.

To understand how He can completely give us His righteousness but still evaluate our servanthood, remember that He is God and we are not. As I have mentioned, He has many aspects to His character. The number of aspects to His character are like the seemingly countless facets of a diamond. He is at the same time the Lamb of God and the King of Kings. As he is the King of Kings, we are His servants, and as a good King, it is appropriate that He rewards His servants who are found to be faithful servants of the King. Remember that heaven is a *real* kingdom where the king rules absolutely. This is what many of the parables are about.

At the same time, He has forgiven us all our sins and has no righteous anger toward us. He evaluates our servanthood and Christlikeness for our eternal place and responsibility in heaven, but He is not angry at us if we didn't do well. He leaves our servanthood and the pursuit of rewards entirely up to us. He still loves us with an unending love and desires for all of us to receive His maximum blessing. He invites all of us to be the faithful servant who multiplies His kingdom ten times. So our lack of sin has nothing to do with our salvation but only our rewards in heaven.

Knowing that there is a large difference in rewards in heaven motivates me to be used by Him as much as the Holy Spirit enables me. We each have a measure of the Spirit, and He just wants us to use all that we have. Some people have more, some have less, and that is OK. We are only responsible for what we have. This knowledge of rewards also encourages me to walk away from sin, not because He condemns me for my sin or is angry at me, but because He will reward me for being more like Jesus. Once again, this is nothing I can accomplish in my flesh; I just need to yield to the Holy Spirit daily to take control of my life and to supernaturally empower me to be like Jesus. I know that in my flesh I still have nothing to offer and am completely dependent on the Holy Spirit.

Paul gives us encouragement in grace and in good works: "Now may our Lord Jesus Christ Himself and God our Father, who has loved us and given us eternal comfort and good hope by grace, comfort and strengthen your hearts in every good work and word" (2 Thess. 2:16–17). He also says, "Do you not know that those who run in a race all run, but only one receives the prize? Run in such a way that you may win. Everyone who competes in the games exercises self-control in all things. They then do it to receive a perishable wreath, but we an imperishable" (1 Cor. 9:24–25).

There is so much more to biblically explore on this topic. The most insightful explanation I have read of the judgment of the believer in the light of grace and rewards can be found in the second half of Rick Joyner's book *The Final Quest*.

CHAPTER NINE

What about Ananias and Sapphira?

If grace is true and we have the righteousness of Christ, then how could the Holy Spirit kill Ananias and his wife Sapphira in the book of Acts after they lied to Peter about how much they had sold a piece of property for?

The believers expected Jesus to return soon. Luke, who wrote the book of Acts, said, "For there was not a needy person among them, for all who were owners of land or houses would sell them and bring the proceeds of the sales and lay them at the apostles' feet, and they would be distributed to each as any had need" (Acts 4:34–35).

Ananias and Sapphira sold one of their properties, kept a portion of the money and brought the rest of it to the apostles, claiming that it was the full sales price of the property. Keeping a portion of the sale was not the problem but rather that they lied about the sales price. Each was struck down dead in front of Peter and "great fear came over all who heard of it" (Acts 5:5).

It is commonly assumed that Ananias and Sapphira were saved because they were part of the group of believers and because they gave this gift. Also, great fear came over the other believers because, assuming Ananias and Sapphira were saved, they feared the same consequence could happen to them. But there is no direct statement in Acts that they were saved or not saved. There are indications that Luke (the author of Acts and the Gospel of Luke) believed that they were *not* saved because he referred to them in a way that is different from how he referred to other people who were believers in Acts.

Here is how Luke refers to the couple in Acts 5:1 and 7: "But *a man* named Ananias, *with his wife* Sapphira, sold a piece of property, . . . *and his wife* came in" (emphasis mine). At first glance, there seems nothing unusual about the way he refers to them here. However, when Luke refers to believers in other passages, he says something to indicate that they are believers. With nonbelievers, he gives them common descriptions such as "a man."

Let's look at how Luke specifically refers to believers in Acts. For the sake of brevity, we will look at references in chapters 1–12, but Luke is consistent through the whole book in this:

2:44 "And all those who had believed"

4:32 "And the congregation of those who believed"

4: 36 "Now Joseph, a Levite of Cyprian birth, who was also called Barnabas by the apostles (which translated means Son of Encouragement)"

6:8 "And Stephen, full of grace and power"

8:2 "Some devout men"

9:1 "any belonging to the Way, both men and women"

9:10 "Now there was a disciple"

9:32 "the saints"

9:36 "there was a disciple"

10:23 "and some of the brethren"

11:24 "for he was a good man, and full of the Holy Spirit and of faith"

11:27 "some prophets came down"

11:29 "any of the disciples"

11:29 "the brethren living in Judea"

12:1 "some who belonged to the church "

12:17 "the brethren"

This is how Luke refers to people who had not yet believed in Jesus:

3:2 "And a man"

3:12 "Men of Israel"

5:25 "But someone came "

6:9 "But some men"

6:11 "they secretly induced men to say"

8:9 "there was a man"

8:27 "there was an Ethiopian eunuch"

9:7 "The men who traveled with him"

9:33 "a man named Aeneas"

10:1 "there was a man at Caesarea"

10:17 "the men who had been sent by Cornelius"

Luke consistently provides a clue that a person is a believer in the way he refers to them (e.g., believed, devout, disciple, brethren). If they are not believers, he uses neutral language to describe them (e.g., man, men, someone).

How Luke refers to Ananias and Sapphira is completely consistent with how he refers to nonbelievers. In Acts 5:1 Luke's wording in describing the couple as "a man named Ananias, with his wife Sapphira" demonstrates that Luke believed that they were not saved.

A second piece of evidence that Luke was convinced they were not saved is found by looking at the verses immediately preceding the introduction of Ananias and Sapphira, where Luke describes Joseph, who he believes was saved, not because he was a Levite, but because he was called "Son of Encouragement (Barnabas)" by the apostles.

Joseph also sold a piece of land and brought the money to the apostles. Luke contrasts him with Ananias and Sapphira in this way in Acts 4:36–5:1: "36 Now Joseph, a Levite of Cyprian birth, who was also called Barnabas by the apostles (which translated means Son of Encouragement), 37 and who owned a tract of land, sold it and brought the money and laid it at the apostles' feet. . . . 5:1 But a man named Ananias, with his wife Sapphira, sold a piece of property, and kept back some of the price for himself." In verse 5:1, Luke transitions from the story of Joseph to the story of Ananias and Sapphira using the word "but." Luke is contrasting Joseph, who was a believer and was honest about the sales price, with Ananias and Sapphira, who were not believers and were not honest about their sales price.

Determining if they were saved or not is important because if they were saved, then the Holy Spirit's response of killing them doesn't seem to fit into other passages that the Bible teaches about grace. Because there is significant evidence that Luke believed that they were not saved, then this story is not contrary to grace.

CHAPTER TEN

Other Questions about Grace

These are questions I have wrestled with when studying what the Bible says about grace. Some of these are very large topics that have been debated for years and have had many books written about them. My goal here is to give a brief perspective on each:

Why then does the Bible say that God disciplines the believer?

God disciplines those he loves (Heb. 12:4–11). This is done for training, not as punishment for our sins and not out of anger. All punishment for our sins was taken by Jesus on the cross. Discipline is for our benefit and out of His love for us. It also results in a greater reward in heaven for us. He is showing us, while we are still on earth, where we are going off the path of service to Him and love for Him and others. This is much more gracious than giving us correction at the judgement of the believer after death when it's too late.

What about the letters to the churches in Revelation? Don't they include judgment of believers?

John received a revelation which he wrote down and in which Jesus had specific messages to seven churches. The messages, while having many encouraging things to say in them, also contain corrections and faultfinding.

For example, Jesus says to the church in Ephesus, "But I have this against you, that you have left your first love. Therefore remember from where you have fallen, and repent and do the deeds you did at first; or else I am coming to you and will remove your lampstand out of its place—unless you repent" (Rev. 2:4–5).

Jesus is manifesting His character here mainly as the head of the church (Eph. 5:23) rather than as the Lamb of God. As I mentioned previously, He comes in different ways at different times, showing different aspects of His character.

A good leader gives course corrections along the way. In Jesus' active role as head of the church, He would thus give direction and corrections to it along with warnings of impending disaster. He loves the church, and He gave Himself for it (Eph. 5:25). The church in Ephesus had lost its fervor of love for the Lord. Jesus' reference to removing the lampstand probably refers to that church's losing its effective role of being a light to a lost world.

This correction is for the Ephesus church's benefit like discipline is. He is revealing the truth of their current condition. A prudent person would receive this. As Proverbs 12:1 says, "Whoever loves discipline loves knowledge, But he who hates reproof is stupid."

But their sins are still all forgiven. Jesus, who paid the price for their sins, is the One giving this correction to them. Why would He want to diminish the work of justification He did for them since He paid the whole price for it?

What about other commands like "husbands love your wives"? Do we do that only when empowered by the Holy Spirit?

Jesus said, "If you love Me, you will keep My commandments" (John 14:15), and His main commandment to us is "to love one another" (John 15:12). So we might obey a command like "husbands love your wives" out of our love for Him and love for our spouses, and we can ask Him to empower us to do this better. It is basically about being in agreement with what He commands and asking Him to empower us to do it.

If I'm living under grace, do I still need to tithe?

There are at least two possible views. I lean toward the first one.

1) We are not under the Old Testament law anymore, and there is nothing in the New Testament that restates a rule of giving a tenth of what we earn back to God. We are now free to give as the Lord leads, empowers and enables us. Paul affirms this idea where he says, "Now this I say, he who sows sparingly will also reap sparingly, and he who sows bountifully will also reap bountifully. Each one must do just as he has purposed in his heart, not grudgingly or under compulsion, for God loves a cheerful giver" (2 Cor. 9:6–7). He is affirming two important ideas here about tithing: 1) it is your choice and 2) don't do it under compulsion but only if you can do it with joy.

2) The tithe is pre-law and is thus a timeless principle. Abram was the first to give a tenth of what he had to God (Gen. 14:20). This was long before the law was given to Moses. But note that he did this voluntarily and not because he had been commanded to do so by God. But Jesus affirmed the principle of tithing by directing: "Then render to Caesar the things that are Caesar's; and to God the things that are God's" (Matt. 22:21). Jesus is saying that the tithe *belongs* to God, not us.

Does Jesus need to be Lord of my life for me to be saved?

What if I were to say that I have made Jesus Lord of my life, and then one day I found a small area of my life that I realize I had not turned over to Him—an area where I was still doing what I wanted rather than what I know Jesus would want? Does that mean that I wasn't saved up to that point? How would I ever know for sure that I have given Him lordship in every little thing? What about when I sin? At those times, Jesus would temporarily not be Lord of my life, but this does not mean I become "unsaved."

Adding lordship as a requirement for salvation is essentially adding a work or a performance standard to the simplicity of receiving salvation as a gift by faith alone. Jesus has completed all work on the cross needed for us to receive salvation. We do not spiritually perform in order to receive salvation. This is what grace is all about.

As we have briefly looked at in chapter 8, many of the sayings and parables of Jesus that look like lordship is required are talking about rewards in heaven for the believer instead of salvation.

Can I lose my salvation?

If salvation is received by grace through faith and without works, then it cannot be lost by a lack of works or even a subsequent lack of faith. If I was required to maintain a certain level of faith or works in order to continue to be saved, then how would I know if I was ever doing enough? Once we are saved, we are adopted sons and daughters of the King (John 1:12; Gal. 3:26). He does not disown us. Our justification is complete for all time. It does not get revoked because of anything we do or do not do. If I have to do something to maintain my salvation, then Jesus' work on the cross was not enough.

CHAPTER ELEVEN

Conclusion

Forgiveness and righteousness are ours by freely receiving them from God through faith in the sacrifice of Jesus. All of God's righteous anger at our sin was placed on Jesus at the cross. We have met all the requirements of righteousness to enter heaven. We have also met all of the righteous requirements of the law.

Jesus did the great exchange when He took our sin on Himself at the cross and gave us His righteousness as a gift. The Spirit is in us, and we live by the new way of the Spirit instead of the old way of the external law.

The Holy Spirit never accuses, convicts or condemns us of our sins (but Satan does), and our fellowship with Jesus is not broken when we sin, because we are already forgiven and justified. When we sin, we can simply thank God that He has already forgiven us. We are not continually falling short of His acceptance because of our sin.

These truths radically set me free, and I pray that they have a revolutionary impact in your life also.

Take a Second Look

When I first learned about grace, I did not immediately "get it." Experiencing life-changing freedom from these concepts does not always happen immediately. These ideas often take time to think and process through. If you feel that you are not yet set free but want to be, then consider reading this relatively short book again. Ask God to show you what the truth is, and then come to your own conclusions. Your freedom may be just one more book read away.

Living in the Light of Eternity

Jesus is the King of Kings of a *real* kingdom in heaven with very different levels of rewards for believers. These truths do not discourage me but rather motivate me to live my life for Him and not for my temporary desires on the earth. I am motivated to use all the gifts of the Holy Spirit that He has entrusted me with. I want to bear fruit for His kingdom, which I know I can do only when the Spirit supernaturally works through me. We are here on earth for just a blip in time, but what we do affects our reward level for eternity.

We can completely wait on Him to lead us into what He is doing and then walk in His power. It's not our role to come up with ministry ideas that we think would be effective. Living in this freedom makes His yoke light, because He gives us ideas and the supernatural empowerment for what He has called us to. No work that we do in our own strength will be God's best for our life and the kingdom. It's a waste of time and results in burnout.

God loves you and is *for* you. He loves to see the Spirit manifest the love and power of Jesus through you to a lost world. You are like Jesus on the earth as the Spirit of Jesus lives in and through you. Jesus said, "In that day you will know that I am in My Father, and you in Me, and I in you" (John 14:20).

His kingdom rule is here on the earth right now whenever anyone comes to Him for salvation and when He supernaturally heals people's lives. This makes what happens in heaven (where everyone is healed and everything is restored) also happen on earth. We can then pray as Jesus instructed us, "Your kingdom come. Your will be done, on earth as it is in heaven" (Matt. 6:10).

He is calling you to live life not in bondage to guilt, condemnation and continually focused on sin, but in the freedom, direction, and power of the Spirit. He is calling out, "Come to Me, all who are weary and heavy-laden, and I will give you rest" (Matt. 11:28). Take the chains off! He has already broken them. Be set free!

ACKNOWLEDGMENTS

Special thanks to my brother Dan Geisler and to Gary Cantwell for their very thorough reviews of the manuscript and countless suggestions for improvements. Huge thanks to my best bud Rick Carnett who has traveled this grace road with me since 1992. I am grateful for his and Joe Quillin's valuable feedback and Bryan Dworshak's feedback and cover design. This work has been immensely improved due to everyone's suggestions.